MIRYAM OF JERUSALEM

Teacher of The Disciples

ANN JOHNSON

AVE MARIA PRESS   **Notre Dame, Indiana 46556**

About the Author:

Ann Johnson currently lives and works in Jerusalem. She is the mother of five grown children and a graduate of Northwestern University and Antioch College.

Miryam of Jerusalem is the third of a trilogy offering contemporary readers a unique and fresh experience of Mary, the mother of Jesus. The previous titles are *Miryam of Nazareth* and *Miryam of Judah,* also published by Ave Maria Press.

© 1991 by Ave Maria Press, Notre Dame, IN 46556

International Standard Book Number: 0-87793-442-8
                                     0-87793-441-X (Prbk.)

Library of Congress Catalog Card Number: 90-84356

Printed and bound in the United States of America.

Acknowledgments

I am grateful to the William F. Coolidge Foundation for a month of research time as a Coolidge Fellow in Cambridge, Massachusetts.

. . . to Rabbi Ben Beliak. As the resource person on Judaism at the Coolidge Colloquium, Ben read and critiqued not only this manuscript but all the previously published Miryam material in order to insure continuity and direction. As a Jerusalem fellow, Ben continued to offer encouragement and guidance during my year of work in Jerusalem.

. . . to the Sisters of Our Lady of Zion. The Canadian Province offered me housing during a year of Hebrew studies in Toronto. The Center in Rome sponsored my research in Rome and Jerusalem. The Sisters in Jerusalem opened their archives and took the time to tell me the oral history of the excavations of Ecce Homo. Another sister arranged for me to extend my stay under the auspices of the Ratisbonne Jewish Studies Program with the University of Toronto funded as Rudun Scholar.

. . . to the editors at Ave Maria Press who welcomed me at the offices on the campus of the University of Notre Dame for several days of work in consultation with them.

For my mother
Vivian Claudia Petrie Johnson

Contents

INTRODUCTION
Miryam Teaches
Yesterday and Today

The early church certainly knew Mary as teacher of the apostles. In the sacred artistic texts of the basilicas and churches of Rome she is still visible instructing her twelve attentive students. The Basilica of St. Mary Major shows her sitting on the seat of distinction in Jerusalem, teaching, arms gesturing, a scroll open on her widespread knees.

In some scenes, Peter and Paul sit at her feet — Peter, key at his waist, Paul, pen in hand, scribbling diligently. She is pictured preparing and directing them toward Rome where the viewer sees the lost pagan citizens, languishing and lecherous, sprawled on their capitol steps awaiting a word of salvation.

In virtually every artistic record of the Dormition of Mary during the first thousand years of the Roman church, twelve eager scholars with books and scrolls open, are depicted clustering around the bed of their beloved sage as she teaches them with her last breath. In most pictures of the Assumption in that same period, she leaves behind her twelve despairing students, clutching open texts to their breasts, holding out scrolls to her, weeping in their loss. So too is she portrayed in her Crowning in Heaven, as those she has just left sit amongst their scattered manuscripts.

The tradition of Mary as scholar lives in canvas, fresco, and stone sculpture. In St. Peter's Basilica, on a vast canvas above a papal tomb, she ascends the steps of the Jerusalem Temple, a young maiden with prophetic bearing. Like Samuel, she is surrounded by devoted loved ones who lend her joyfully to instruction and God's service. She is received by a saintly High Priest, resplendent in simple white garments and ephod, who represents the Twelve Tribes. Holding out a warm and welcoming hand he escorts her to her place in the Temple school for prophets and Levites, such as the Prophet Huldah maintained in her day.

Artistic records of her childhood are exclusively of her schooling. She sits at the feet of her mother, Anna, on the lap of her kinswoman, Elizabeth, in Hebrew school, or in a teacher's presence. As a mother, she is remembered as the teacher of her son. She whispers to the nursing infant, murmurs in the ear of the toddler standing on her lap. She reads to the Holy Family when they pause on a journey or rest playfully in a garden. The young Jesus leans against her knees while she instructs him.

These paintings, frescoes, and sculptures of Mary as teacher may seem surprising to Christians today. Beginning with Constantine in the fourth century, much of Western Christendom was swept up in the powerful euphoria of Byzantine Christianity. For example, in places like Ravenna, Italy, where we know the Jerusalem church was strong, all the artistic texts were covered over by magnificent glittering mosaics of the divine Theotokos and her Son, the Christos. Lost with the artwork was a sense of Miryam as teacher of the apostles.

As we have seen, however, the footprints of the Jerusalem church are unobscured in Rome. There we witness a community that blends the church of the circumcised and the church of the gentiles. The marble floor of St. Mary Major Basilica still retains two massive six-pointed Star of David inlays, one on each side of the altar. The six-pointed star also graces many windows and archways and hovers over sacred scenes.

The early followers of Jesus in Rome observed Jewish ways. For the most part they worshiped and worked with devout Jews of the Italian tradition. The Jewish community, established and thriving at least one hundred years before Jesus' birth, was well respected by Roman citizens and visitors. The practices of the main body of Jews and the Jewish sect of Nazarenes were so similar that people often confused the two. Tombstones and catacomb graffiti place them side by side.

While Jews and Romans lived and worshiped together in Rome, the presence of Romans in Jerusalem was often a source of tragedy for the Jews. Roman legionnaires, soldiers far from home, not fighting but drawing unimportant and boring occupation duty, often played sadistic games. One we might call "get the bride first," in which betrothal records were bribed or extracted by terror from Temple officials and the young women raped. Another we might call "walk a mile," where any Jew could be commandeered to carry a pack or serve as a lackey with accompanying jibes from a soldier — but only for one mile because Roman law was "just." (Both Jesus and Hillel teach us to "walk with them two miles," hoping to show the mystery and courage of a people of God.) John the Baptist is beheaded in a fatal banquet game. History held a place for the Jews and Christians of Rome in a grisly sporting arena with gladiators and lions.

In Jerusalem, archaeologists have uncovered and restored the tic-tac-toe grid of the gruesome "Game of Kings," a game board scratched on the pavement that once covered the courtyard of the Antonia Fortress. Arrayed around the etching are the symbols of slave nations present in Jerusalem from which the fatal selection would be made. Prominent among them is a six-pointed star to indicate the possible selection of a "king of the Jews" as their pawn in the game. A throw of the die cast the rules of the game and determined the group to be singled out. Its leaders were ordered to provide a "king" for whom the people then voted. This king was hailed, tortured, humiliated, and led up the hill to be crucified. Pilate didn't believe in over-interference with his troops' entertainment. Perhaps the Game of Kings gives a clue to the strange events of Jesus' passion, the mock trial about which so many scholars raise their unanswered questions. Perhaps this discovery will provide a key to facts that somehow do not seem to fit. I have woven these possibilities into the story portion entitled "These Are the Things We Did."

Jerusalem itself was destroyed by Roman armies in the year 70 of the Christian era. Even its name was blotted out from the nations as Hadrian later titled it Aelia Capitolina, combining the familiar pagan Saturn Capitolina with his family name. He is reported to have sown the soil with salt so that it would never again bear fruit. In 135 C.E. Hadrian forbade use of the name Judah or Land of Israel, replacing it with Palestine for the Roman goddess Palestra.

The Jews never ceased passing on their memories of more just societies in their past — just societies called for in the prophets' writings and created by some of their monarchs. Both first-century Jewish sages and the Nazarenes held out hope of living again in their very lifetimes in a reign of an anointed one like David, another Messiah. In this great day a just peace would be established for all times, never-ending, a reign when many were perfect, when sinners returned to God, when the Land provided for everyone and no harm was done "on all God's holy mountain." In this time of hope our stories take place.

Our story speaks of the period when the Temple still stood and the newly formed band of Nazarenes thrived. Church tradition tells us that Mary lived fifteen years in the Jerusalem community. Jerusalem flourished. The Nazarenes were one religious group among many. Many vital communities within Jewry lived various forms of communal life in towns and villages. We read of *Kesherim*, the blameless ones; *Anawim*, the humble; *Hasidim*, the pious, apparently the origin of many early followers of Christ. Documents also list *Zenuim*, the chaste; *Hashaim*, the silent; *Vatikim*, firm-principled ones; *Kadoshim*, saintly ones; *Bannaim*, the builders of God's reign; and *Anshe Ma'sheh*, doers of miracles. Wilderness monasteries were equally varied and unique.

In Israel of this period women as well as men read from the Torah scrolls in synagogues and houses of study. They prayed often with phylacteries and presided as celebrants and sages in the community at Sabbath tables. Women and men served together, a nation of priests according to the Pharisaic teachings that all creation reflect God's glory. Women's names appear along with men's as leaders and members of ancient synagogues. All these activities drove St. Jerome to lament years later, "The trouble with Jews is that they give their women too much freedom!"

We have further confirmation of communal celebration from Jewish records dating from the second century of the Christian era. A rabbinic sage of the period exclaims, "Every scholar in the Land prizes an invitation to the Sabbath Table of the great sage Beruriah" (Talmud). There in Tiberias by the Sea of Galilee Beruriah taught Torah all Sabbath night in her home until the hour of morning prayer.

In the year 70 when Rome destroyed Jerusalem, reducing the Temple to a heap of blackened stones, Jews continued praying in the ashes. Beginning in 135, the terrible agony of Jews in their sacred Land intensified as Rome suppressed the final struggle of Bar Kochaba. The Roman occupiers made teaching Torah an offense punishable by death. Jews were deported from Jerusalem; no Jew was allowed within the city gates. The acts of Roman state terror — murder, burnings and public torture — fill the annals of Jewish martyrology and the histories of the period such as those recorded by the church father Eusebius.

In this period after 135, Rabbi Judah formulated the three blessings in preparation for the forbidden and dangerous study of Torah every morning. In order to fortify themselves for the terrible choice between teaching Torah and death, or not teaching Torah and staying alive, they prayed these prayers:

I.   "Blessed are you, our God Sovereign of Creation,
        who has not created me a Gentile"
            (that is, not knowing Torah).

II.   "Blessed are you, our God Sovereign of Creation,
        who has not created me ignorant"
            (that is, not capable of understanding Torah).

III.   (Women pray) "Blessed are you, our God Sovereign of
        Creation,
            who has created me according to thy intent"
                (that is, specifically commanded to choose life).

    (Men pray) "Blessed are you, our God Sovereign of
    Creation,
        who has not created me a woman"
            (that is, not specifically commanded to teach
            Torah).

This third blessing, which is so controversial in modern times, emerged from the political reality of the danger of teaching Torah, rather than an attempt to limit women's rights and dignity. In public, where one could be recognized and singled out for immediate execution, only men read Torah. Women were not forbidden to read Torah in public, but they were not commanded to do so. On the other hand, all men were so commanded, both to protect the tradition and to hold accountable those men who might assimilate into the dominant culture of the area.

Much of the separation of teaching Torah into male and female tasks in public worship may be understood as emerging from this period when Jews were torn between the need to worship God according to their covenant and the need to survive in order to do so. In the home, where the essence of biblical Judaism is celebrated, women are the celebrants and transmitters of the tradition. Only a woman can initiate the Sabbath as she images God's initial creative act by kindling lights.

Archeological discoveries have unearthed a rich treasure of the last desperate attempts of the pursued to hide their personal possessions and sacred texts. They bear witness to the age of Israel before Western conquest. The legal papers of the matron Babatha, now housed in Jerusalem's Shrine of the Book with the Dead Sea Scrolls, testify to the contractual and witnessing power of women in practical Jewish law. Her contracts are displayed, some of which are written in her own hand and witnessed by her with the required corroborators. Babatha buys and sells property, contracts marriages with full protection of financial independence for the woman, and conducts business with other men and women in the community.

Confirming the antiquity of Jewish women's rights and responsibilities are the documents of Jewish Elephantine in Southern Egypt. There, in the sixth century before the Christian era, papyri record women who brought their own legal action and acted as their own attorneys. This invited the ridicule of the resident Greeks who said that the Jews didn't even provide competent counsel for their women. The court records currently available show that Jewish women trained in Torah study served as successful attorneys regularly defeating their Western counterparts in court.

In light of these many documents, we begin to understand our own story of the Christian community in the New Testament. Jesus leads a group of both men and women in which women were valued as providers, teachers, witnesses, and leaders of houses of gathering. At no time did the Sadducees or Jewish religious leaders ever challenge Jesus on the presence or even prominence of women among his disciples.

The text of this book is divided into three portions: *Study*, *Prayer*, and *Daily Living*. In each section, we can hear Mary speaking to her community, to the followers of her Son, teaching them in the traditions of their people.

The first portion, *Study*, summons us into the heart of the biblical tradition. The words and commandments of the Living God to Israel are carried forward from generation to generation in the stories of her people. The promise to tell the stories and teach the Way is still reaffirmed every day in Jewish prayer: "You shall love your God with all your heart, with all your soul and with all your resources. Let these matters be always upon your heart. Teach them thoroughly to your children and speak of them to one another while you sit in your home, while you walk on the way, when you lie down and when you rise up" (Dt 6:6-7). In telling stories people not only become centered in their personal religious identity but find guidance for the challenges of their own lives.

The Bible is the foundation of Judaism. Scholars tell us that the oral tradition is rich and imaginative. Through the reading of texts and the telling of stories the teachings are pondered day and night. We also now know that in teaching, women often told the stories of the biblical women, and men told the men's stories, because each could contribute unique insights and personal testimony with the authority born of like gender. As Mary tells the stories of women in the Hebrew tradition, we find her own story echoed in the telling.

The early church bestowed upon Mary several names by which we honor her memory and seek to know her. Among the earliest names are Wisdom, Our Mother, Highly Favored Woman, Mother of Sorrows, Queen of Peace, and City of Refuge. All of these names are known in the Jewish tradition of her day as the attributes of specific biblical historic women. The attributes the Hebrew community ascribes to Eve, Sarah, Hannah, Mother of Sorrows, and Queen Shalom-Zion give us some insight into the attributes the gospel community accords to Mary when they name her with the honors traditionally given to these women.

Eve

Eve's story is told in the first four chapters of Genesis. She is portrayed as the original woman. I have drawn on the Bible's own written text as well as earlier rabbinic sources such as *Genesis Rabba* to tell her story.

While scholars postulate two creation accounts, in Mary's tradition there is only one. In Genesis 1—2:4 the verbs describing God's actions have qualities ascribed to architecture. From there on the verbs suggest actions by a builder or potter. The verb for the creation of Eve is that of an artisan, an embroiderer. Thus the functions of the creative process are delineated, from the inspiration and planning, through the construction, to the final essential artistry. The story culminates in God's success in bringing forth a vital continuing creation, complete with living icons of the very God-self who have memory, can make choices, and have chosen to know the difference between good and evil. Like God, they are able to bring forth bread and life, experience pain and intimacy, engender strength and vulnerability, establish justice and mercy, make mistakes and recover from them to create again.

Understanding this mythic religious poem depends on understanding its symbols. The symbols are linked to a particular geography. For instance, the serpent is symbolic of divinity, wisdom, and royalty in the territory east of the Mediterranean and in Egypt. The serpent is an ancient sacred metaphor for the servant of God. The Jerusalem community brought this symbolic understanding to Rome, where holy wisdom in the ancient form of the serpent is still visible in artistic representations of Jesus as Servant of God. Entwining a cross, lifting its head from a chalice, or encircling the Tree of Knowledge, the serpent represents Word or Torah, inviting believers to risk everything on God's teachings. In Eastern symbolism the serpent's challenge generates spiritual growth, healing, resurrection. The biblical text supports this interpretation throughout. Note Exodus 4:1-5, where the serpent-entwined staff becomes the rod of Aaron and Moses' leadership, and

Numbers 21:6-9, where the fiery serpent challenges the Israelites to have courage and acts as the instrument of their resurrection from the dead.

Understanding the living traditions of Genesis also requires familiarity with the geography of Jerusalem and her modern holy sites. Judaism, Eastern Christianity, and Islam regard the great rock on Temple Mount as the foundation stone of the world. The rock is known to all three religions as the rock of Abraham's proving by God. The rock was part of the holy of holies in the Temple in Jesus' day and is the focus of the Moslem Dome of the Rock today. In the Holy Sepulcher church there is a room called the Tomb of Adam. Surrounding the old city of Jerusalem is the valley of the dry bones, and all three religions have burial grounds there. All these sites spring from the Genesis story.

Some Hebrew words in the Eve story occur only in that context. Others are translated and interpreted differently in that story than in any other place in the Bible. In translating the story for this text I have chosen to use meanings generally accepted throughout the entire biblical text. Thus, the word for *pain* is translated strength, *cursed* becomes separated, *cunning* becomes prudent and so on.

A manuscript used by Rabbi Meier in the late first century is much quoted and contains similarities to the spiritual teachings of the scriptures. I have used two references to this manuscript. The first is that God gives life and death, and both are good. The second is that God clothed Adam and Eve in tunics of light. Both interpretations are based on valid readings of the Hebrew.

As the Genesis text underwent translation and interpretation for the Western Greco-Roman people it took on the acculturation of their mythology. The story in modern Christian understanding transmits an impression which more closely resembles Pandora's box than its original intent. Understanding it from Mary's first century perspective can enlarge our awareness of God's creative action and blessing in the world.

Sarah

Sarah's story is in the Book of Genesis (11:27—12:34). She is, and was always, respectfully and lovingly called Sarah, Our Mother. I have drawn on biblical commentary of the Anchor Bible series, Rabbinic writings, and the research of Savina Teubal's work on Sarah and ancient priestly women, as well as Raphael Patai's classic volumes on *Family Life in the Bible* and Ginsberg's *Legends of the Jews*. This story raises painful questions of inheritance and nationality, family unity, and separation. These were issues for the gospel community and they are issues for us today.

Sarah is the pivotal figure who carries her priestly tradition to a land God chooses. She is charged with the miracle of a child and the awesome responsibility to raise that child according to the unique and mysterious direction of their God. Abraham and Sarah and Hagar struggle with God's promises. All three are called prophets in the Jewish tradition. Each of them receives the teachings of God directly in holy experiences.

The central issue of separating ourselves and our children in order to restrict certain influences and enhance others is a part of our lives also. This woman who dares to separate her family, enduring pain and the judgment of the ages, is portrayed in all her prophetic fullness as the woman who sowed the seeds of religious courage in Egypt that would bear fruit in the lives of Pharaoh's daughter, the midwives, the mother of Moses, and Miryam the prophet as they set the circumstances for a separation, the Exodus, from Egypt. All these events are foretold in the Genesis story of Abraham and Sarah.

Hannah

Hannah's story is told in the first chapters of Samuel. Hannah, highly favored woman, is considered a prophet and the founder of prayer as we know it. She is God's faithful servant. She sees violence in the religious sphere and commits herself heart and soul to its correction. Her story is a paradigm of the faithful believer. The Christian community cherished this tradition, and Mary's Magnificat is a memorial drawn from the model of Hannah's prayer.

What does Hannah mean when she declares, "I lift up my horn of praising"? Our Latin and Greek translations render the word "horn" as spirit or soul. Ancient Jewish meditations on this single word are abundant. Since it is so much a part of Christian tradition I have included several of these definitions in the prayer.

Hannah describes God as a being like a garment, a shadow or shade, like a tent, an enclosure, a rock, and a refuge. All of these descriptions figure in the gospel and epistle accounts. She speaks of resurrection from physical death by God and of resurrection from spiritual, psychological, economic, social, and political death by divinely inspired people doing God's work. The original Hebrew text is a radical testimony of the empowerment of God available to humankind. Hannah's prayer and her life story cannot be separated. They are the root, the flowering, and the fruit of one another.

I have let the images called forth in the original language fill out the prayer in an effort to communicate some of the world view this biblical perspective defines. The symbolic forms used in the Latin or Greek translations indicate a world "sitting upon columns." The Hebrew touches our deepest consciousness describing creation as hovering over a flowing watercourse, a contained primeval chaos. Our literary river Styx or the hymnody "down by the riverside" reflect these ancient Hebrew archetypal images.

Mother of Sorrows

The Mother of Sorrows story is taken from the Book of Second Maccabees. It is told also in the noncanonical books of Third and Fourth Maccabees. Much has been written about the political situation in the Land of Israel during the time of Jesus' ministry and the early church. Scholars and theologians continually call our attention to the impact these circumstances had on the New Testament writings. In the last half-century the church has again reassessed these writings and the results of that re-examination are reflected in many modern biblical commentaries.

Two aspects loom so large in church deliberation that they merit reference. First, discoveries and scholarly developments have enabled proper interpretation of documents, historical texts, economic records, travel diaries, and personal journals that detail the vast and extensive brutality of the Roman Empire. From Britain to India, Egypt to Syria, history affirms the witnesses recorded in Maccabees, Jewish martyrologies, and histories of the church fathers. Scholars now acknowledge that Christian need for self-preservation influenced the pro-Roman, anti-Jewish writings in the New Testament. Second, the bias of the New Testament has resulted in an interpretation of gospel events that has had tragic consequences in the long history of the church. In the Vatican II document *Nostra Aetate* (1965), the church directs us to cease the teachings of contempt for Jews and search for the truth.

John 10:22 records that Jesus went up to Jerusalem for the Feast of Dedication and it was winter. Records show that the story of the Mother of Sorrows is a central theme for this feast. We also know that the early church used this text as the liturgical reading for the Marian Feast of the Mother of Sorrows. In the Eastern Catholic churches, this heroic Jewish martyr, mother, and sage is also a saint. In this Maccabean text the church preserves the only record of Pharisaic teaching on the doctrine of the resurrection as a theological teaching. The Mother of Sorrows is the theologian.

Queen Shalom-Zion

Queen Shalom-Zion's story is recorded in the annals of Jewish history, in both the *Antiquities* and the *Wars of History* of Flavius Josephus, and in royal documents of neighboring states. She was an ally of Queen Cleopatra VII of Egypt. Christian historians of the later period tend to dismiss her reign because she waged no wars of acquisition. She is a historical figure listed in our biblical indexes of Hashmonean monarchs by her Greek name Alexandra Salome. She reigned over the Land of Israel from 74 until 67 before Christ. The heightened expectation that a messianic society was possible in real geopolitical time is based largely on Israel's experience of her just and generous reign.

She is still known as the Queen of Peace and City of Refuge. Testimonies to Shalom-Zion's holiness and God's response to her righteous rule were displayed in the Temple precincts during Jesus' lifetime. Records say that samples of the overly large grain, lentils, and nuts that the land bore in her time were preserved for all to see.

Wisdom Teachings

Each woman's story ends with words from the Wisdom writings. The great feminine presence of God is named Wisdom in the Bible. Mary is the Wisdom figure teaching the church. Teachers in the Wisdom tradition know and love the Bible and treasure its words in their hearts. Many of the women's stories emerge in the sacred metaphor of the Wisdom books. We find them in Proverbs, Ecclesiastes, Ben Sira, Ruth, Job, Song of Songs, as well as in the Psalms and Daniel.

In study and prayerful familiarity with the Bible one begins to experience the wonder of the Bible teaching about itself. Wisdom ponders her own treasures, reflecting on her own stories. She examines a moment from this way and that. She inquires and sings and imagines. Hearing Bible stories told in the authentic Wisdom tradition from the mouth of Mary, Wisdom of the Church, liberates our listening and empowers us to grow in faithful knowledge.

The Magnificats of Prayer, found in the second part of this book, are based on the prayer of Israel, which is modeled on Hannah's prayer. This prayer of Israel was prayed three times a day, although some prayed them once or twice. Eighteen biblically inspired sacred themes, developed over a course of time, serve as a pathway of prayer in communal and private worship. The prayers themselves are in the likeness of Hannah's prayer, a spontaneous outpouring of the heart within an ordered structure.

The order of the prayer themes sometimes differs from community to community, although the first seven are fairly stable. I suggest that we probably find remnants of this prayer practice in our own Christian community. The addition to the Lord's Prayer appears to match the first three blessings: the kingdom, the power, and the glory. It is possible that these words were a cue to begin the longer prayer of Israel, or a short form of the prayer itself. There is another familiar note in the direct affiliation between confession and the acceptance of forgiveness followed immediately by physical healing. This relationship also appears prominently in Jesus' ministry.

The order of the eighteen blessings is as follows: three praises (ancestors, God's power, and holiness), thirteen petitions (responsibility, repentance, forgiveness, redemption, healing, harmony, ingathering of exiles, justice, protection, fidelity, messianic age, acceptance, and joyful service) and two prayers of thanksgiving (gratitude and peace). Each prayer is a necessary prelude to the one following it. Each prayer is an outgrowth of the spiritual integrity experienced in the one before it.

Daily Living, the third portion of this book, explores the life of Mary as a founding member of the Jerusalem church. The Book of Acts clearly places her within its center. We have seen how church tradition remembers her fifteen years of work as its matriarch and teacher.

I have also selected traditional thoughts and teachings from each of the New Testament writings that are fundamental to the Christian message. These passages have often been preached and taught from a perspective alien to Jesus' teachings of inclusive love and to his heritage as a faithful Jew. Drawing on the work of theologians and pastors who have labored to transform our understanding of some of these difficult passages, my intent has been to remain faithful to both the letter and the spirit of the text.

In every age the church has continued to tell her founding story in liturgy, song, sermon, theology, and statements. The challenge remains: How do we live in daily life the heritage Jesus bequeathed?

Christians today face a special challenge in understanding the reality of Jesus' incarnation as a faithful Jew living two thousand years ago, born in Bethlehem in Judea. The specifics of time and place, of culture and geography, shaped his teaching. Brought up in Galilee by parents who observed the Jerusalem Temple customs, Jesus taught and healed in the hill country around the lovely harp-shaped lake in Galilee. In Jerusalem he endured a terrible death and was raised to life in God according to the resurrection belief of his Jewish tradition.

As modern Westerners, we have not always found it easy to follow this teacher whose heritage is so different from our own. Sometimes it seems as though it would have been more reasonable if God had chosen another place, another time, and another person for an incarnation. Perhaps we experience a greater affinity with Plato or Alexander the Great, perhaps even Gandhi. But no, Jesus is the One, and so we humbly seek to come into his tradition on God's own terms.

As an author I hope I have told the story well. Wherein I have misunderstood and been mistaken, the fault is my own. Wherein I have perceived the truth, been challenging and sensitive, I am grateful to a searching church and her many servants and especially to her wise and constant mother, Mary, Teacher of All Christians.

PART ONE: STUDY

Miryam speaks,

    teaching the apostles,

        teaching the Jerusalem community,

            teaching the followers of her Son today.

Jerusalem, My Jerusalem

Miryam speaks:
>   Jerusalem, heart of the world,
>   Jerusalem, core of creation,
>   Jerusalem, my Jerusalem.
>   I stand here now where my ancestors stood.
>   I behold this Rock, this Mountain Moriah, this Temple Mount.
>   This is the substance on which the world is founded,
>   the very center of our history,
>   the sanctuary of our memories,
>   the source for all who seek to know the Living God.
>   Jerusalem, my Jerusalem.
>   From this dust, we were taken for life.
>   To this dust we return in death.
>   In the time the Almighty chooses,
>   this dust will rise up and live again in glory.

Before time began, when Chaos reigned, God spoke and Chaos attended. God made everything and set it spinning. God made every being and gave it life. From a spring bubbling up from the deep beneath, God gathered dust, made it moist, and here on this rock the Creator kneaded clay into creatures like the very God-being, breathing them alive with holy spirit, planting a garden called Eden around them.

In the center of Eden, God established the Knowledge Tree, the Tree of Life. Here in this place woman and man first ate its wisdom fruit. Here they realized the holy awesomeness of the Living God, their creator and their teacher. Here they came to know their humble nature. Naked and inexperienced they stood, wise in their fear of God. On this rock they received their great enduring labor of love, to be like God, suffering and working in creation, bringing forth bread and life from dust.

Then God cast them forth upon the land, like fisherfolk cast their nets upon the sea, like farmers cast seeds upon the soil. God cast them eastward to the "land where two rivers meet" facing Eden. There they knew blessing and knowledge and mercy. They brought forth bread and children. And their generations began to call upon the name of God.

Then the time came when God wanted them home. Two thousand years ago El Shaddai called Abraham and Sarah from the groves of Mesopotamia saying, "Move, move away from your land, your kindred, your family property. Go before me into the land which I will show you." And they went before God, spending themselves for a lifetime making choices for God.

Then the time came when God said, "Go up to my rock, my mountain, Mount Moriah. Prepare to lift up your son as an offering and I will teach you how to worship me."

They came here to this very mount, Abraham and Isaac, Sarah's son. Abraham bound a willing Isaac. Then as though lifting up an offering, Abraham laid Isaac upon the altar, upon this rock from which the beginning spark was struck, this rock on which God moulded humankind. God watched them come, seduced by their vision. Surely they would falter. But no, they prepared for death. Such was their awe. This time they stood in Adam's place clothed, fully experienced in life, and they feared enough to honor the vision of God.

"Wait!" whispered God. "Wait!" cried the heavenly messenger. "Abraham, Abraham, here I am! Lay not your hand upon the lad, nor do him any harm, because I see you here. You are clothed in the ways of life, experienced in my teachings, and yet still you have chosen to obey my voice. You stand in holy fear before me."

Abraham lifted up his eyes and beheld a ram caught in a thicket, for surely the vines of Eden were grown thick and wild, untended by human hands. Abraham beheld the ram caught in the thicket and offered it instead. They went out from Mount Moriah and knew the blessing of building generations in covenant in the Land.

Two thousand years we have been in this land. On this Temple Mount humankind first tasted wisdom and stood in awe of God. I stand where God tested our ancestors Abraham, Isaac, and Sarah and found them obedient. I ponder as I gaze upon the hills, knowing it is but a day's walk from here to Hebron, where I go sometimes to sit silent beneath the terebinth trees and pray at Sarah's family tomb.

In the course of time we went down into Egypt. What was begun in humiliation ended in glory. Joseph went down a slave and rose up a steward, grown from the house of Sarah, a mighty redeemer. And according to Sarah's prophecy, Pharaoh set by his side a holy priest of Egypt, the woman Aseneath, to assure salvation from famine, and her name was called "City of Refuge." She united the house of Egypt and the house of the Hebrews and secured the teachings of mercy in Pharaoh's court. Even after, when new Pharaohs came and the deeds of Joseph were forgotten, the seeds sown by Sarah and Aseneath thrived, providing strength for the women of Egypt and securing a sanctuary into which Miryam the prophet delivered the child Moses.

With Aaron, Miryam, and Moses God led us out of Egypt, bringing us home. We were weavers, masons, embroiderers, scribes, artisans, dyers of blue, makers of brick, and architects, musicians, and some of us tillers — all of us slaves in an alien place, all of us cut off from this Land.

God of our Exodus, our hope renewed, our spirits stunned by your caring power, we stood before you in fear in the wilderness. There on Mount Sinai you gave us the Law of Life. You gave us your fruit of knowledge. You asked us, "My people, my people, will you take my teachings?" We answered "Yes" and in the wilderness learned to live as your beloved. When we felt exhausted and abandoned and turned away from you in confusion, you corrected us and we returned.

We rose up, our strength surging. You lifted us high on eagle's wings, flying. You taught us to run and not be weary. You taught us to walk the long walk with you and we came home to the Land of our origin.

We walked long years coming home to this Land. Once here you sent many to guide us. Hannah saw our needs and with you brought forth a prophet who anointed a king and another king. . . .

One thousand years ago King David, your singer, brought the Ark of the Covenant home, dancing his way through the valley before me. He designed a Temple on this rock and his son, Solomon, built it.

Though enemies have encompassed us, burning your Temple, sending your people into exile, though we your beloved have not always been faithful, we have returned. Five hundred years ago a remnant returned from Babylon and built again. Now we are the generation of your helper, Ezra. We return again and again to Eden where the Living Tree bears fruit. Its wisdom fruit is the teaching of Torah. When we eat fidelity and honor from the Torah tree we claim your promise of eternal Life. For you have assured us from the beginning that if we eat from it and fear you, we will live forever. You are the giver of life. You are the giver of death. You are the giver of resurrection from death. You go down into hell with us, accompanying us closely, and in your presence we return to life.

Today I gaze out upon the Rock on which the world was founded, the Mount Moriah, where God sees and is seen. Today I live two thousand years since our return from the "land where two rivers meet."

All this time there have been Hebrews here, tilling these hills, tending these valleys. They thrive, and the abundance of Israel cannot be measured.

Now in my time I walk in these holy places where Adam and Eve first tasted the bittersweet fruit of wisdom, where Abraham and Isaac stood in awe of God. At this altar Rock where they heard words of compassion, I pray. Today I dance in the Temple when my people celebrate.

Jerusalem, heart of the world,
Jerusalem, core of creation,
Jerusalem, my Jerusalem.
I stand here now where my ancestors stood.
Behold this Rock, this Mountain Moriah, this Temple Mount.
    This is the substance on which the world is founded,
        the very center of our history,
        the sanctuary of our memories,
        the source for all who seek to know the Living God.
Jerusalem, my Jerusalem.
From this dust, we were taken for life.
    To this dust we return in death.
    In the time the Almighty chooses,
        this dust will rise up and live again in glory.

Magnificat of Remembering

Sing, my soul of God's extravagance.
Breathe, my being in the perfect freedom of God's love.
For I have been told the tales of glory.
>I have heard the melody of revelation.
>I have felt the gaze of God.
I, a simple, common, everyday woman
>ordained by my Maker in my mother's womb,
>I am a portion of Israel's priesthood.
I accepted God's crown of sacred servitude,
>adorned myself in the yoke of careful attendance.
I will be remembered forever because of these blessings.

The very name of God is Holy.
>Compassion and generosity season God's actions.
>Power and kindness shape God's way.

Remember, my people, remember.
>Those who choose faithlessness are forgotten.
Cherish, my people, cherish the faithful.
Cherish the deeds they performed, the beliefs that sustained them.
Cherish the prayers that they prayed.
Remember and cherish. You, too, may choose God.
May my teaching,
>like teachings of the Living God from the mouth of Moses,
>>come like a desert breeze to enliven your mind.

May my teaching,
    like teaching of the Living God from the mouth of Ezra,
        enter into your substance like the morning dew
            building up the temple of your heart.
May my teaching,
    like teachings of the Living God from the mouth of Jesus,
        anoint you like oil,
            healing and restoring you, body and soul.

Remember, tell your stories day by day,
        pray your prayers along the way,
        return to life and choose God.

THE STORY OF EVE
The Woman Who First Tasted Wisdom

(Genesis 1–4)

Miryam speaks:
Some of you call me "Eve."
>It is true, I am a woman of wisdom.
>I share with you the fruit from the Tree of Wisdom,
>>asking you to discern and decide,
>>to choose between good and evil.

I stand now where Eve once stood.
Let me tell you her story as it was told to me,
>a story I often told my son,
>a story we read from the Torah scrolls,
>a story so steeped in sacred mystery, that we must first
>>tarry an hour in silence with God before we begin.

Like the *Song of Songs*, like Ezekiel's fiery vision,
>this text we call *Beginnings* is a spirit-text.
>Hewn from the vastness of antiquity, whispered voices have
>>echoed round fires in the night,
>>>telling . . . telling . . . telling . . . .

God, who is Light, makes light and gives us the task to enlighten.
God, who is Laborer, makes labor and gives us the task to labor.
God, who is Life, makes life and gives us the task to make life.

Beginnings speaks of the Tree of All-Knowing,
    which is the Tree of Life, our Torah . . . .
    It speaks of the cherubim, great gracious winged creatures
        that still guard the Torah in the Temple today . . . .
    It speaks of a flashing double-edged sword.
        (A prophet once told me it would pierce my heart, and it was
        true — it has. It will pierce yours also if you have the courage
        to reach out and eat from the Tree of All-Knowing.)

And what about Eve?
    She is a mystical figure bent by shadowy storytellers.
    Her name in our tongue is Havah, Life-Giver.
        Listen to her tale.

Beginnings
When in the beginning God began creating all things,
    there was everywhere wanton, wild wastefulness,
        a churning, cold, chaotic bleakfulness,
    and the Awesome One's wind roared,
        swooping over the primeval watery chasm.
Then it began happening!
God speaks a spark into being,
    a flicker breaks open and flares.
God sees. It is good.
Causing a dynamic separation, God sets amber and indigo swaying,
    conceiving of brightness and nightness.
    Evening and morning begin their existence
        becoming, together, one day.
    God creates Time.
God sketches reoccurring rhythms,
    draws details within the grand design,
    a blueprint of a potent promise,

etching ebb and flow, up and down, in and out, thrust and
    pause, clinging and casting forth, life and death,
thereby making possible the sacred spawning of this self-
    sustaining universe.
Yes, it happens in the emerging plan that
    lamps will illumine the sky-vault,
    setting in sequence the celebrative seasons.
    The very earth palpitates and pulses and teems,
    its seed-bearing plants sprouting forth from the ground,
    its water filling with swimmers and drifters,
    its air fluttering with flyers and swoopers,
        some with fiber-wings, some with feather-wings;
        on the land, swarmers, crawlers, stalkers and herds.

There, in the midst of it all, God considers. . .
    considers the possibility of making an entire humankind.
A humankind designed in the amazing pattern of the Awesome One!
God conceives a living icon of the very God-self,
    imaging God's own sacred image and intent.
God creates each of us solitary beings, singular, unique.
God creates each of us kinfolk, a couple to struggle and love:
    Zacar, manly, and Nekavah, womanly, made to fit together.
    Zacar, Rememberer. Nekavah, Choice Maker.
God creates each one of us as endless community.

God endows humankind with this blessing,
        "You are to bear fruit, to be many and changing,
            to complete the earth, filling it up.
        Inhabit my place and make it your home.
        Govern it as I would, make it my footstool,
            the place where I rest. Make it my house, my delight.
        Here it is! Take it please. I give it all to you. . .

every seed-bearing plant upon the face of the entire earth,
every tree and its tree-fruit bearing seeds of its own kind.
These shall be your food. Food for everything that lives,
    the flyers and swimmers, the crawlers and swarmers,
    the wild rovers and the gentle herds.
Amazing! O yes, this is exceedingly wonder-full.
    Behold, it is good to live.
    Behold, it is good to die.
    Behold, it is good to continue forever in your company.
      You are all my holy attendants."

God rested from the great euphoric enterprise and
    named the rest-time Sabbath, a holy time.
God and all the sacred company rested together,
    setting the Sabbath like a crowning jewel upon a diadem,
    deep within the dynamic design they had been doing.
    Together they stopped the doing and rested.

Continuing

Then, after rising up from the rest and coming forth, the generator of heaven and earth, a laboring, begetting God, began plying the sacred design, taking up the shaping, the moulding, the form, constructing the earth from scratch.

When in that time shrub-stuff had not yet been cast forth nor herb-plants because God had not yet caused rainfall, because humankind had not yet been fashioned in its final form, a surge welled up from within the earth, a fresh blessed stream bubbling up from beneath the dust, moistening the entire surface of the ground.

God pressed the moist earth, sculpting and shaping a God-perfect image from the mud, then blew into its nostrils a rush of life. The holy icon became alive, living-dust in the image of God.

We were one vital being, healthy, and fraught with divine destiny, manly and womanly, remembering and choosing.

Then God planted a pleasant place called Eden, a garden of delight, setting humankind within it. And God caused every kind of foliage to spring forth from the ground, every tree desirable to the eyes and good for food, including the Life-Giving Tree in the center of the garden, the Tree of Knowing-All-Things.

All we know about stewarding the earth and each other, all the good people have done in every age, we learned here in Eden. Our God was our teacher.

First we learned to work, to till, to tend, to guard, and protect the living things. Then we learned to eat from the fruit of the earth. From every tree we were to eat freely, except one. The fruit from the Tree-of-All-Knowing was not free. God feared for us, saying, "When the time comes that you eat from it, surely you will die."

God saw our aloneness. "A human being alone is not good. I will make a worthy partner."

From dust God formed all wild-life and flyers, bringing them hopefully one by one before us, to see what we would sense about the essence of each. Whatever we called it, that was its name.

But among the beasts there was none to be a worthy partner, no helper corresponding to our own unique intent. There was no beast equal to the task knit into our bones.

Therefore, God, the skillful physician and great artisan, cast upon our single being a profound sleep, a dying from which only God could waken us, a sacred soma, and in that trance, we were seized by God, lifted up and broken open, separated side from side.

One side, Zacar, was skillfully repaired, the woundedness sealed, healed, closed over. A perfect creation.

One side, Nekavah, was built up, knit new, her spirit beautifully braided, her soul embroidered upon. A perfect creation.

God beheld Nekavah and called her Ish-ah, Woman. The sages say God took great joy in the building up of Ish-ah. Then we were awakened.

There in the Garden of Delight, God brought forth Ish-ah, in tender mother love like a father brings a bride. The waking Zacar saw her, and seeing, realized himself. Seeing the woman, the man understood.

He repeated her name, "Ish-ah," and in it heard his own. "I am Ish, Man," he cried, "and she, she is the one. We are bone of same bone. We are flesh of same flesh. We are taken out of one another.

"Because this is how we are created, a man must always leave his parents' home and come into the home of his woman, clinging to her there in faithfulness, holding fast, reuniting again to become one form, like God."

And they were vulnerable in each other's presence, unclothed, knowing secret things and sacred mysteries, and there was no confusion back and forth between them.

Fulfillment

As things developed at a later time, when the serpent had become prudent, indeed more sensible than any beast made by God, it said to Ish-ah, "Is it indeed true that our God has said to you that you are not to eat of every tree in Eden?"

Ish-ah replied, "From the garden fruit trees we may eat, from this fruit tree here in the midst of the garden, God said not to eat from its substance, and indeed, we do not even touch it lest we die before our time."

The serpent said to Ish-ah, "Surely you will not die aforetime, because God knows that on the day when both of you eat from its substance, you will be aware. Your eyes will open. You will become fully God's true likeness, realizing everything, from all that is good to all that is evil."

Ish-ah acknowledged that it was a goodly tree to eat from, delightful to eyes that seek wisdom, desirable in order to show oneself fit for true understanding.

She took its fruit. She ate, giving it to her Ish at the same time, and he ate also.

When the eyes of the two of them were opened, they were able to distinguish between good and evil, a complete revelation. They perceived all possibilities: happiness and misery, leisure and labor, celebration and destruction, loving and lechery, learning all things as God knew them.

Astounded by wisdom, they realized their vulnerability. Stunned by reality, they were awed and afraid. They were humbled, but they did not die.

Lovingly they reached out and plucked leaves. Sewing together foliage doubled over, they made tunics for themselves, protecting and shielding one another.

Then, they heard the sound of God moving back and forth in the garden during the breeze of the day. Ish hid himself and his Ish-ah in the midst of the trees, awed by presence of God.

God called out, "Where are you?"

He came up before the face of God, saying, "I heard your sound in the garden. I shuddered. I trembled. I was afraid because now I have perceived how vulnerable I am. And so I hid myself."

"Who revealed to you that you were vulnerable? Ah, I see, it is from the tree-fruit that I instructed you not to eat. Have you eaten from its substance?"

Ish confessed, "Ish-ah, who you gave me, handed it to me and I ate."

God spoke to Ish-ah. "Tell me what happened."

She responded, "The serpent challenged me to lift it up and to eat."

God told the serpent, "Because you arranged this revelation, you will no longer be bestial. You will be separated from beasts and wildlife.

Like a twisting cord you shall move about all the days of your life binding and unbinding, sustained by dust which is the human essence. You and Ish-ah, your descendants and her descendants will strive together, always struggling with essential questions. To know or not to know? To become wise or remain naive? To grow or to languish? You are the awakener of existential inquiry, ethical integrity, and spiritual thirst. You are the 'niggling question,' and they will strike at your head to drive you away, but you will always be beneath them, striking at their heels."

God explained to Ish-ah, "Now I will increase your strength. Now you too will be a laborer in creation, a begetter of human-kind. Now you can give birth to living icons. Your man will provide abundance for you and he will be like you."

God told Ish, "Now because you listened to your Ish-ah's voice and ate from the tree which I cautioned you about, you are no longer dust of the ground. The ground will be separate from you. You will cause it to give up its gifts, pressing the dust, laboring in creation just like I do. In your service, you will be a laborer in creation, growing food to eat all the days of your life.

"Thornbush and thistles may sprout up around you, but fields of fresh juicy herbs will be your nourishment. You will sweat, it will drip from your nostrils, but you will always have bread to eat. And when you die in your proper time, you will come home again, returning to be rejoined with the ground, because from her I myself lifted you up. My dust you once were, my dust you will become again."

Woman and man had truly become image and likeness of God, fit to continue creation with God in an eternal partnership.

Then the man of the earth saw the sacred essence of Ish-ah, his woman-side. He proclaimed her new name, Havah, Life-giver, or Eve, as the Greeks call her. She had become, like God, a life-giver. She is the source of everyone who lives.

Now, at this time, the Living God, the laborer and the begetter, made tunics for the man of earth and his Ish-ah. God, the Living God, clothed them both in light. They were clothed in clothing made for them by the Living God.

Seeing them emerge complete, God spoke, "Look, behold humankind is truly alive. Indeed humankind is made from our very same substance, knowing all things, both the good and the evil. Now, it is I who am filled with awe! I fear their hand may seize even more substance from the Living Tree and they may eat from it, becoming alive even to the hidden wisdom."

So God commissioned humankind: "Move on. Separate from Eden. Serve the earth, all of which was taken from here. Serve the earth, which is called Adamah." From this the Ish sensed his essence and took his name, Adam.

Like fisherfolk casting a net, God cast forth the human beings. Like a farmer sowing seeds, God cast them east of Eden, facing toward it. God settled the holy cherubim of blessing before Eden. They were gracious great winged creatures. God also established the mystical flame-sword, the whirling, flashing double-edged sword in order to protect the pathway to the Tree of Life.

Creation Sustained

After all this happened, Adam, full of knowledge, made love with Havah, his wife, and she conceived. Here, east of Eden, facing the place of creation, they were blessed.

When she gave birth to a child, she saw his sacred essence and she named him Laborer, in our language, Cain. She lifted him up, proclaiming, "I have created a human being, just like God!"

She continued to increase, bearing a full brother, seeing his essence, and she named him Vanity, Abel. Abel became chief of the flock, Cain a laborer, an earth-tiller. In their adulthood they came one day to serve God.

Abel brought what seemed a perfect sacrifice.

Cain brought what seemed a lesser one.

Cain despaired, his face fell.

God instructed him, "If you do a good and pleasing thing, lift it up. When you do what is not good, carelessly, when there is no pleasure, you open an entrance and there is sin. For carelessness is a croucher, lusting after you. But you can master it."

He did not master it, but murdered his brother, whose name was Vanity. The first sin! Terrible! Brother taunting brother over ritual perfection. Brother slaying brother in religious jealousy.

God saw the act and caused justice to begin acting in the world. Cain appealed. God listened and heard and caused mercy to begin acting in the world. God set a sacred seal upon Cain in order that no one should harm him because he was already judged by God and the receiver of God's compassion.

And Cain went forth, chastened and restored, a laborer, building cities. From his stock came tent dwellers, stone masons, metal workers, musicians, and skilled crafters. From him came forth Lemek, an ignoble warrior. From him came forth Namah, the righteous wife of Noah.

As for Havah, full of knowledge, she made love with Adam and she bore another child. Seeing his essence she named him The Appointed One, Seth, because, she said, "God has appointed to me another harvest instead of Vanity whom Laborer slew."

To Seth there was born a child named Humility, Enosh. From that time on the generations of Havah and Adam began to call upon God by name.

This is the book, the scroll telling of the generations of humankind. In the day that God created humankind, in the likeness of God were they made. Man and woman, God created them, and blessed them and called them by name, humankind. This all happened in the age when they were created.

Our sages say, "There is unity for humankind in the image of God. There is reverence for the divine in the image of one another."

Israel remembers the woman Eve. Each Sabbath evening, here in our homes, at the table we call a holy altar, we read again from the sacred scroll the story of that first Sabbath.

Come. It is commanded. Men, leave your parents' home. Come into the homes of your women. At the altar of blessing, woman presides, kindling light as God once did. Here the bread that I offer you is the bread of Eve. See I have built it beautifully, woven it into a crown like a bride's crown, braided it down like an old woman's hair. Lovingly, I have built our bread, in honor of the way God built woman.

Eve is a woman sated with delight choosing creation, shaped, built, honed in the substance of the Living God.

The Book of Holy Wisdom teaches us wisdom: "My children, never turn away from God's formation nor take offense from such reproof. Those whom God loves are carefully set upon the right path. God shapes sharply the beloved offspring.

"Happy are those who have claimed wisdom, who have acquired understanding. She is the staff of life to all who grasp her, the tree of life to those who hold to her steadfastly.

"My children keep watch over your skills and your prudence, do not let them slip from sight. Observe your father's examples. Do not turn away from your mother's teachings.

"Instruction is a lamp, Torah, a light.

"The first step to wisdom is the fear of the Living God. Call wisdom your kindred, understanding your best friend, knowledge your holy bond. Those who fear the Living God shall live. Choose life, that you may live."

THE STORY OF SARAH
Prophet, Matriarch, and Sage

(Genesis 11–24)

Miryam speaks:
Some of you call me Mother.
>It is true I draw you to myself in love and mother you.
>It is true I seek to nurture you
>>and keep you separate from alien influence
>>>in these your formative years.

I stand now where Sarah once stood.
Let me tell you her story as it was told to me,
>a story I often told my son,
>a story we read from the Torah scrolls.

This is a tale of three prophets: Sarah, Hagar, and Abraham. Listen well to the story of Sarah, our mother.

Sarah's Place of Origin

When you walk toward the morning star, eastward from the rock of Temple Mount around which Eden our beginning place was planted, crossing the great Aramean plain, you come into the "land where two rivers meet," Mesopotamia, and a great city there called Ur.

Long ago before this was the Babylonia of our exile, before this was the city of a single sovereign law, before the great stepped temples were built — long ago this gentle land bred gentle people. They were wise and peaceful, gifted and God-knowing (though God was known by many names and often seen in idols, which is different from our way today).

Beginning in this place so fertile in our history, is the ancient culture, and we, through Sarah, Rebecca, Leah, and Rachel, are its daughters.

Centuries before Sumer swept down upon her, Mesopotamia, the "land where two rivers meet," was not bound together in nation-statehood but was instead a collection of peoples clustered in religious centers.

Some built temple cities, great stretching structures whose form fit the land, expansive in function, serving every need of civil law and worship.

Others simply set their sacred cities in godly groves, equally exquisite and expansive, fostering a powerful and generous tradition. The date-palm, Tamar, the oak, Terebinth, the cedar and olive, also trees fruited and fragrant, all bore witness to the gifts of a caring creator. Priestly sages generated justice, excellence, and artistry. Tented there were the vast temple schools and libraries, clay tablet records, psalms, and histories. Tented there were shelters for the stranger, the refugee, the wounded and sick.

The grove sages were priestly women, living lives of simple daily holiness. It was believed their presence caused the land to blossom and yield according to the people's needs. It was said of them often, "You are a blessing in the land." The witness of our texts gives evidence that Sarah lived the vowed life of a grove woman. Indeed, the texts indicate that she was one of the first among them, for her name is Sarai, "Woman Prince of God's People," and her kinswoman was Malkah, "Sovereign Woman." From these two are our people descended.

Mesopotamia was a cradle of civilization then. In time hordes came from elsewhere with great plundering armies. The hoarders came lusting to pick the plum of civilization nested in the branch between two rivers, to graft their civil and religious priorities upon her ancient tree. These were nation builders. "One way for all," they said, "one language, one law." Hewing down the living groves, the living traditions as well as the living beings, they made way for those who put stone on stone, constructing against the form of land, building their high temples, steps-up-to-god. Their juttings crumbled as the living earth pulsed and quivered with the offense. They failed, of course. Confusion overtook them and they became babblers in a city of Babel from whence Babylonia received its name, but their civil laws survived and still serve there.

Sarah, Woman Prince of Ur

Terak, a northern chieftain, kinsman to Sarai, came down with his sons Abram and Nahor to gather his own from out of the ruin. He saved them from the Babblers, and Sarai united with Abram, Malkah with Nahor. They returned north to Terak's family holding in Paddam-Haran.

The ancient grove monasteries of Paddam-Haran welcomed the holy women who fled there. Sarai continued as a consecrated priest and accordingly tradition tells us she was a sage, a brilliant scholar, a mover of mountains. She was without a child, of course; the land and its people were the children of these sacred sages. Their blessing bore fruit in hospitality and wisdom, justice and compassion. Their blessing bore fruit in enoughness.

Sarai never requested a child. Her womb was sealed, her will bound to God.

Childless we live deeply in this world,
    available now for the work of this day.
Childful we live spread over time,
    past and present and future.

The good our people have done in every age, the good we do here in Jerusalem in these times, is our inheritance passed on from the hands of Sarai. Amongst the Terebinth oaks so generous of shade and shelter, so giving of healing herb and holy incense, the tented women dwelled as God-servants devoted to the land and its inhabitants. The grove was all that a God-house could be and the priest-women were the God-hands, the God-heart, the God-wisdom, and the God-power.

Here were libraries, learning, and artistry.

Here were healers, dream-tellers, festal celebrants.

Here was refuge, sanctuary, and court.

Here the treasury, storehouses, and markets.

These holy women were called "fair to look upon." Spirit-filled, their goodness cast forth from their faces like light.

Herders of herds great and small brought the first and finest of their flock as thank offerings, building to perfection the temple flock, reserved for God and the refugee, reserved for the poor and the well-intentioned wayfarer, reserved for the servants themselves. And these women priests were the Temple shepherds.

Tenders of fields great and small brought the first and finest of their harvest fruit as thank offerings, building to perfection the temple storehouses, reserved for God and the refugee, reserved for the poor and the well-intentioned wayfarer, reserved for the servants themselves. And these women priests were the Temple stewards.

Builders of buildings great and small brought the first and finest of their skills and stones as thank offerings, building to perfection the Temple wells and cisterns, reserved for God and the refugee, reserved for the poor and the well-intentioned wayfarer, reserved for the servants themselves. And these women priests were the water drawers.

So it was with poets and weavers, with scholars and potters, with dancers and singers of songs, each bringing their best as a thank offering to the Temple grove where the women priests received them. Here in the sacred Terebinth groves the great and the simple, the land dwellers and the nomads, even the well-meaning wayfarers received the hospitality of heaven, received hospice, refuge, and sanctuary. Mercy was meted out in ample measure. Here in retreat sacred dreams were dreamed, their meaning discerned. Here visions were seen and embraced. Here seekers heard and recorded in clay the very voice of God.

The great chieftain Abram came also bearing his offering, giving thanks and seeking wisdom. Now God spoke to Abram saying, "Move, move on away from your homeland, from your kinfolk and from your family household, toward a land that I will show you. There I will make you a great nation. I will support you and confound those who seek to lessen you. My blessing will be upon you and your name. Because of you all the families of humankind will also experience my blessing."

Accordingly, Abram rose up. With Sarai and Lot, his brother's son, he prepared to set forth. Together with all their substance and all the souls they had acquired they went out from Paddam-Haran, forward toward Canaan, and into the land of Canaan they came. Two great households they were, the household of Abram, a chieftain of Paddam-Haran, and the household of Sarai, Woman Prince of Ur.

They passed through the land to the sacred place at Shechem where there were the Terebinth Oaks of Morah, that is, the Teaching Oaks or the Terebinth of Seers, for religious people of the Canaani dwelled this land.

God appeared and spoke again. Abram built an altar to mark the place of God's teaching in the Grove of Shechem-Morah.

They continued to a mountain-house of God, Beth-El, where they paused. But there was no source of blessing living in this land and the Canaan was fraught with famine and besieged by drought, so they descended down into Egypt.

Sarah in Egypt

Nearing Egypt, Abram feared for himself, his substance and his people. He traveled over toward Sarai's caravan, approaching and seeking her protection. He addressed her, "Behold, most fair woman. I am afraid! I fear that when the Egyptians see you and your royal household they will realize your priestly power. They will judge that I and mine are nothing but a husband in your court and do away with us quickly.

I pray you confer upon me the title of priestly brother. Tell them I am blood of your mother's blood. In that way they will spare my life and honor me because of you."

So it happened, as the two caravans arrived at the border, princes from Egypt seeing the woman prince from Ur and all that was hers, sent a spirited message to Pharaoh regarding her presence. She was escorted directly to Pharaoh. Abram received the protection due her, and she set up her residence in Pharaoh's court.

But the ways of the priests of Ur were not the ways of the Pharaohs of Egypt. God-servant and god-king clashed, sowing revolution in the royal city. She did not become a wife in Pharaoh's regency. There was no political alliance, no confiscated goods. Her ways were a plague on his house. Her fast-won followers were many, including Pharaoh's own magnificent daughter, Hagar.

Pharaoh knew he must rid his court of this Sarai, this disturbing Prince of Ur of Chaldees. He must do it and save face besides.

Pharaoh and his princes went out to Abram's settlement. Heaping upon him a flurry of wordy accusations and a cascade of rich gifts, he pled that they be gone with both their houses. The sages tell us he gave to Sarah the Goshen territories northward, which Egypt at that time held, and there they were to go and settle. And they say that before Sarah journeyed up from Egypt she cast forth this prophecy,

Someday there will rise up from my house a man who will penetrate Pharaoh's court. This seed I have sown will bear fruit. He will become like me, an establisher of sacred storehouses. Someday all peoples will know what we know and there will be built up houses of blessing in the starving land.

"Patriarchs will rise from the ranks of the poor and the rich alike, and the power of matriarchs will be reclaimed. And there will be assigned to the side of this man from my house a woman from the house of Pharaoh — a mighty woman who will unite the people of Egypt with our people and her name will be called 'City of Refuge.'"

Sarai went out from Pharaoh's court. At her right hand went the young Hagar, woman-prince of Egypt.

Sarah in Hebron

Together Abram and Sarai came up out of Egypt, very wealthy in cattle, in silver, in gold, increased in the souls of their households. They came up, returning north to the sacred places where God could be heard and listened to. Following according to the visions, they settled across from Kiriath-Arba, now our city Hebron, in the sacred Terebinth Grove of Mamre. Here Sarai set her tent. Here she was welcomed and established herself and her house, sharing her wisdom and goodness amongst her neighbors. She taught and healed, welcomed the well-intentioned wayfarer, accepted thank offerings and dispersed them fairly, building a household of respect and peaceful ways.

Abram too gained the respect of his neighbors as he set about the work of his God. He possessed the land not by conquest but by covenant. His work proclaimed itself in wells and words of justice and peacemaking. Ten years Abram and Sarai labored in the land.

The sages say that the spirit of God filled Sarai's tent just like it fills the Holy of Holies. They say a light shone forth from it by night and a cloud hovered over by day. Fire and mist shadowing Mamre drew all things to her house. They say that from her tent the goodness of God was cast forth.

So much so that years later, at the time of her dying, all the elders of the region grieved with Abraham, offering him the gift of a large burial cave facing Mamre, for her bones to rest among them forever. But Abraham purchased the land as a resting place for all their generations. So it was that he too was laid beside her by Isaac and Ishmael, their sons that they loved. Also laid to rest there are Sarah's generations after her. Today in the Hebron cave of Machpelech the bones of the Matriarch Sarah and her descendants rest beside Abraham, the Patriarch. All the while the matriarchs served in the tents of Mamre there was blessing in the land and there was no famine or drought.

Sarah's Household

In time Hagar, too, became "fair to look upon." A favored child of Egypt, she matured at Sarai's side. Ten years, the scrolls say, she served beside Sarai, learning the ways of the sacred women. Cloistered at Mamre in Sarai's care, she became a worthy inheritor.

Abram desired a child of Sarai's line. He would not wed a wife of alien gods.

Sarai was stopped from bearing. God had set a sacred seal upon her womb. But Hagar, her right-hand woman, was not restrained from bearing. Hagar, raised up in Sarai's house, was schooled in the way of the steward. Hagar was willing and so it was that Sarai placed the hand of Hagar, the Egyptian, in the hand of Abram, the chieftain of Paddam-Haran. Hagar became his wife and mistress and Abram did as Sarai instructed him, believing together they would bring forth a child which would increase the house of Sarai and fulfill the promise of God to Abram.

Hagar conceived. Her body filled up with a prince descended from generations of grandeur and audacity. Filled up with the presence of a mighty child drawn from the power of pharaohs, drawn from the might of the chieftains of Terak.

Fed on Abram's expectations of greatness, Hagar grew large and became her own woman. Hagar swelled up with pride, turned away from grove-woman ways. Her back to Sarai, she claimed another prize.

Sarai raged against Abram. "In your tent! In your lust for greatness you have spawned this betrayal!" Then Sarai prophesied, "God will choose. God will choose between us. God will choose, your way or mine!"

Stunned, Abram responded, "Here, I return her. Take her to yourself again to be your right hand, to teach her as you will."

Sarai tried to retrieve her, pressing her ever harder, but she pressed against the grain of Hagar and Hagar rose up and went away from Sarai, returning toward Egypt the way she had come.

She reached the well of Shur. Drawing water there, God's messenger spoke to her, "Hagar! Hagar, Sarai's own woman, where have you come from? Where are you going?"

Hagar responded, "I have turned away from the face of my master Sarai and I have fled."

God's messenger said to her, "Return. Return to your master and bend, bend beneath her strength. Many, many will be your seed and they will not be numbered among ordinary people. Behold, you are with child. You shall bear a son and you shall name him Ishmael, One Heard by God. God has heard your distress. He shall be a wild ass of a man, his hand on everyone and everyone's hand on him. He is to dwell to the east of Egypt where his kindred dwell in the full presence of them all."

Hagar called God "The Speaker God Who Is a Seeing God." To this day the well of Shur is known as Beer-la-ha-roeh, "the well of the one who lives and sees." It is located in the Negev, south of Hebron, east of Egypt.

Hagar returned to her master Sarai. She bore a son and brought him to Abram. Abram named him Ishmael, according to Hagar's vision.

Twelve years passed. God appeared before Abram, saying, "I am El Shaddai. Walk in my presence and be perfect. I will make a covenant between me and thee and many will grow out of you, increasing and increasing."

Abram fell down on his face. God talked to him for a long time. "Here and now, I covenant with you. You will father a murmuring crowd of nations. Therefore, your name is no longer Abram, Exalted Father, but Abraham, Father of My People. I will bear fruit to you again and again and monarchs will come forth from you. I establish my covenant between us and those who grow up out of you. I am your God and their God. This land in which you sojourn, I give to you, to hold in the palm of your hand forever. Our covenant sign is to be etched in the flesh of each male born or brought into your house."

Sarah the Matriarch

And God said to Abraham, "Sarai, your wife is not to be called Sarai, Woman Prince of God, but her name is Sarah, My Woman Prince, Power of Yah. I bless her — I give to you a child. I bless her — from her nations shall come forth, monarchs of peoples. She shall be the wellspring of nations."

But Abraham, who had fallen on his face, laughed. He said in his heart, "A child of a hundred-year-old man? And with Sarah! A ninety-year-old woman giving birth?"

Therefore, Abraham said to God, "Ishmael is the one who lives before you."

God corrected Abraham. "Sarah, it is Sarah, your wife, who will bear a child and bring it to you and you will call his name Isaac, One Laughs! With him I will establish my covenant, with him and those who grow out of him forever!

"As for Ishmael, I have heard your request and I will bless him also with fruitfulness and multiply him. Twelve tribal chieftains will I give him for children in the place where he lives and they will become a great people.

"But my covenant, etched in your flesh, my covenant I establish with Isaac, whom Sarah will bear at this time in the season to come."

God finished instructing him, and went away from Abraham.

Immediately, Abraham took Ishmael, his son, along with the males of his household and circumcised them.

It happened one day that God came to the Terebinth Grove at Mamre. Three figures appeared. Calling, "Adonai," Abraham rushed from the entrance of his tent to arrange hospitality. First, he ran to Sarah asking her to prepare the bread of offering.

Sarah took three measures of first-fruit flour for the offering bread. She skillfully kneaded it and deftly spun it on her whirling fists, chanting prayerful rhythms as she crafted the large flat round loaves. Slapping them on the oven stone, they bubbled up, steaming fresh aromatic hisses. Flipping them quickly, she finished and held them out to God.

The three figures sat before Sarah at the table of blessing. Abraham brought his portion, and stood to the side of the guests. Sarah was in the entrance of her tent. The guests ate the meal.

Then they said to Abraham, "Where is Sarah, your wife?" He replied, "She is right there! Look! In the entrance of her tent."

The visitor announced, "I will return. I will return to you in the season of life-giving. And behold! Your wife, Sarah, will have a child."

Now Sarah listened, standing in the door of her tent. The way of women had ceased in Sarah and her very womb laughed, rejoicing.

"Shall the delight of women be within me again? I am old, Adonai, old."

God said to Abraham, "Why this! Sarah laughing, saying within her, 'Truly shall there be a birth and I, so old!' Is anything too wonderful for God? I say to you there is a season of life-giving and Sarah will have a child!"

Suddenly Sarah trembled, terror struck, weakening, "No," she cried, "No, I laugh not! I am afraid!"

The messenger reassured her, "No, Sarah, you will laugh, rejoicing."

The visitors rose up from Mamre and looked down upon the face of Sodom.

God causes life. God causes death.

From Sodom we learned that one man, one family, is not enough to sustain goodness alone. Sodom teaches us that ten, at least, are required. Ten must stand together for righteousness.

Abraham woke up in the morning and saw Sodom's smoke from the hill of Mamre. Afterward, he went down to the Negev and dwelt there, saying of Sarah, "She is my sister."

But God heard him and restored all things in Sarah's behalf.

God visited Sarah. God did unto Sarah according to the word. Sarah conceived and gave birth to a child. Sarah brought forth a son for Abraham in his old age.

Abraham called Sarah's son Isaac and circumcised him at eight days according to the covenant.

Sarah spoke, "Truly God has made my laughter. Everyone who hears of this will rejoice with me. Who ever would have told Abraham that Sarah would nourish a child at her breast!"

And the child grew.

For the customary years Sarah fed her child, completing his growth and training him up. She nourished him in her own way.

When the time came to wean him away from his mother's side, Abraham staged a great feast. There was laughter and rejoicing, daring games on horseback, dances and a great drinking festival all arranged by Abraham. Hagar the Egyptian and Ishmael their son were there.

Ishmael was now a strapping youth, a budding wild ass of a man . . . bold, brash, grown gallant on the surface, but still a boy within. He laughed, playing the field — the horses, the games, the women.

Young Isaac could not take his eyes off this great wild ass of a man. He vied for favor of his elder half-brother, worshiped, adored this beloved son of his beloved father. Ishmael continued his games, playing here, playing there, then he turned and began playing with Isaac.

Sarah saw them.

Sarah the Prophet

Our sages say that in that moment all her gifts of prophecy came clear. Sarah gazed into a future and saw this lad of the desert and her lad of the grove growing up together. She saw her house crumble beneath the flamboyance.

"Enough! No! Abraham separate yourself from this mistress and her son, because this mother's son shall not take possession over my son. He shall not control my Isaac."

Abraham wept, driven to despair by his sons' divided destinies.

But God spoke to Abraham, "Weep not over the youth or over your mistress. Everything that has been said to you by Sarah, do it! Listen to her voice! Because it is through Isaac that I will summon your generations. I will also cause the son of your mistress to become a nation, because he is your seed."

Sarah gazed into the future. She saw the love of Abraham, Hagar, and Ishmael. She saw the love her little Isaac bore them. Often Abraham and Isaac would journey south to be with them. And the brothers would stand together at their father's grave.

Sarah instructed Abraham kindly and he did each thing she said. Rising up early in the morning, to make a start before the sun was high, he placed ample bread and water skins of fresh water on Hagar's shoulder and the lad's. Bidding farewell, Hagar departed on the caravan way toward Egypt, as she had done before.

Sarah gazed into the future and she saw that the great house of Hagar would someday come to the rescue of the house of Sarah. Their lives were forever entwined. She saw her distant kinsman Joseph, the dreamer, drawn up from a pit by Ishmaelite traders and taken down to Egypt, there to fulfill what she had begun.

Hagar journeyed, but she went astray into the wilderness of Beersheva, the well of Abraham's covenant. When she and her son finished the water from the water skins, she left the lad under a tree, for his bravado had caved in and he wailed and she could not bear his distress.

But God heard the lad and God's messenger cautioned Hagar not to be afraid, to get up, pull the lad up and sustain him with her strength, for he was to be a great nation. God opened her eyes and she saw the well, went, filled the water skin and gave the lad a drink. God accompanied the lad, settling him in the desert. He grew. He dwelt in the desert and became a great bowman. He stayed in the south, east of Egypt, where his mother brought a wife out of Egypt for him.

Many years later it came to pass that God called Abraham up to the rock to prove him, establishing with him forever a sign of our people. Alone among all our neighbors we do not sacrifice our sons and daughters on an altar of offering. This was the proving of Abraham and this was the proving of Isaac.

Our sages say Isaac came to Sarah, his mother, after he had been to the mountain of God's appearance with his father, Abraham. Isaac rejoiced because he had known God's compassion face to face. He had known his own willingness to be a sacrifice for God. Bound, he had lain upon the altar, and with his own ears he had heard God's "No!" From this day forward Abraham is known in our stories as "the friend of God," but Isaac is known as "God's kinsman."

Like Isaac, we follow our fathers, who follow their God, and rely on God for our redeeming.

Sarah knew her work was completed and she rested from it. Sarah died.

Her tent was empty of her spirit. The sages say the light died with her and the cloud covered Mamre in mourning. Grief settled upon Hebron.

After the placement of Sarah's bones in the cave, after the time to mourn was completed, Abraham saw that Isaac was ready to inherit the covenant. He sent his trusted right-hand servant Eliezer to his home in Paddam-Haran. There, Terak had brought the grove women so long ago from the house of Malkah; there, Eliezer, guided by God, would find Rebecca, the water drawer, Sarah's heir.

Sarah's son Isaac was a laborer, a lover, a pray-er of prayers, a man worthy of a woman like his mother. Sarah's tent regained its light and its spirit when he brought Rebecca to dwell there.

Isaac, the son Sarah separated from the wild desert chieftain, became a patient, peaceful man, although he always seemed tempted by rogues. He went often to the place in the south, east of Egypt. The two sons stood together at Abraham's grave. Isaac favored Esau, his rough, tempestuous son, who was a bowman like Ishmael his elder half-brother. Again it fell to the matriarch to secure the painful separation which would insure that there would rise up from the promise and covenant of this people a great nation faithful to the Living God.

The sacred scroll of Wisdom teaches us,
"The creator of the universe laid a command upon me
     decreeing where I should dwell.
"Make your home in Jacob's house,
     find your heritage in the tents of Israel.
"In the sacred tent I ministered in God's presence and in this way I came to be established in Zion. I took root among the people of God's honor, among those of God's possession. Like a terebinth I spread out my branches, laden with honor and grace. I put forth shoots like the vine, and my blossoms were a harvest of abundance and integrity. I gave birth to noble law, to awe, fear of God, to knowledge, and holy hope. I give all these to my eternal offspring, God's people. Surely, I will be afraid of nothing. Nothing is too wonderful for God."

Surely we are all Sarah's children of laughter. Surely we know the difference between being sacrificed and being "like a sacrifice" on the altar of God.

Surely we remember that God spoke to Hagar, but never at Mamre. In her flight to Egypt, in her despair in the desert, God spoke and made promises to her which have been fulfilled. In her son is a great nation. In our teachings, Hagar is a prophet. God saw her mighty in her own place, but God never spoke to Hagar at Mamre.

Each Sabbath eve, here in my home, at the table we call a holy altar, I kindle lamps so that my tent may be like Sarah's "alight with the light of God." In the lamp that I hold in the palm of my hand, pinched of clay, there is a wick in each of the four corners. I light them in remembrance of the matriarchs. One for Sarah, one for Rebecca, one for Leah, and one for Rachel. By this act of lighting I choose their way again.

Each Sabbath eve I bring you bread, as Sarah brought the bread of her hands to God. Together we must seek to be the hands of Sarah, to be as she was, fair to look upon, a blessing to all families in the land.

The Story of Hannah

A Prophet and Greatly Favored Woman

(1 Samuel 1–2)

Miryam speaks:
Some of you call me Greatly Favored.
This is the meaning of Hannah's name.
It is true, I am a woman of prayer.
I have been graced most abundantly by God.
It is true that when I see confusion among you,
like Hannah, I seek God's help to dispel it.
I stand now where Hannah once stood.
Let me tell you the story as it was told to me,
a story I often told my son,
a story we read from the Torah scrolls.
This is the tale of the prophet Hannah.

Hannah was the first person to name God Sabbaoth, Lord of Hosts, in prayer. She foretold the great work of her son, Samuel. He was Israel's wisdom, its priest, its prophet, its seer and anointer of kings.

She foretold the greatness of her great-grandson Heman, the singer. Heman became a horn of praise, lifted up to God and the nations. He was a chief musician in David's Jerusalem, standing on the sanctuary steps, his fourteen children among the singers and dancers.

Heman, Hannah's great-grandson, was called David's seer, and some of the psalms are ascribed to his honor.

She foretold the destruction of Sennacherib, the fall of Nebuchadnezzer, the redemption wrought by Esther, the return of the remnant of Israel from Babylon, and the conquest of Alexander the Greek.

Hannah's prayer is murmured in our homes and synagogues today, taught at our Sabbath table. Hannah was a prophet and mother of prophets. Listen well to the story of Hannah. She is the one who established the pattern and form of our daily praise, supplication, and thanks. She is the fount and foundation of prayerful Israel.

Hannah was loved. Her husband, Elkanah, loved her. She lived in the time of Judges, when pilgrimage to the ancient sacred sites was part of Israel's custom. She lived in Ramah, in the hill country north of Beth-El, and her place of pilgrimage was Shiloh. The whole family went up to worship.

Before we begin, however, we must understand the meaning of their names. Hannah is "highly favored one." Elkanah, her husband, is "one who is owned by God." Hannah had a sister-wife named Peninnah, "the cornerstone." Peninnah had children. Hannah had no children. The family loved one another, and often just the sight of Peninnah teaching her children brought Hannah grief.

It was a time of goodness in Shiloh. The priest sat on the seat of distinction by the gate. His name was Eli, "one who goes up and worships." He knew God.

It was a time of despair in Shiloh. Eli's two sons were worthless lads. These two priests, sons of the gentle Eli, harassed the worshipers. They moved among the pilgrims as they prepared their sacred meal, threatening, bullying, taking more than their share from the offerings. In this way they dishonored the praying people of Israel. The sin of the lads was very great before God. Their names were Hophni, "one who takes with both hands," and Phineas, "one who turns his face." They were not good lads. They did not know God.

Among the families of Israel there was a certain one from Ramah: Hannah, Elkanah, Peninnah, Peninnah's children, and all the household. They came regularly to Shiloh to worship at the temple, honoring the holy rhythm of the celebrative seasons. Whenever Elkanah offered an offering, he meted out the portions to Peninnah, to her sons and to her daughters. To Hannah he gave a portion like them all, because he loved Hannah.

The Living God had set a seal upon Hannah's womb. The very presence of her sister-wife Peninnah, with her children worshiping gathered round her, caused Hannah to mourn. When she went up to worship in the house of the Living God, she grieved, she wept, she could not eat.

Elkanah, her husband, said to her, "Hannah."

She replied, "Here I am."

He said, "Hannah, why go on weeping? Why do you not eat? Why are you so heart-broken? Am I not good to you? Better than even ten children?"

But Hannah rose up and left, left the wine and meal of offering in silence. Like Ezekiel, she went "in bitterness of spirit. In the heat of her spirit, the hand of God was strong upon her."

Now Eli, the priest, sat on the seat of distinction by the door post of the Temple of the Living God at Shiloh.

Hannah, her soul seasoned greatly in mourning, prayed to the Living God. Weeping, she poured out her heart. Standing, her hands spread out before her, she vowed a vow.

"O Living God of Hosts, God of the witnesses of heaven and the multitudes of earth, strength of the forces of Israel, holy warrior, God Sabbaoth, look at me. See my humbled soul. I am your servant. Remember me. Do not cease to care for me, because I am one who serves you. Give to me, please do give to me, for I serve only you.

Give to me a sown seed full of life. Give me a child and I will give the child to you, the Living God. I will set before you a dedicated one, a Nazarite, and all the days of this Nazarite's life there shall be no wine, no strong drink, no razor shall touch this Nazarite's head."

In this way she continued to pour herself out in prayer before the Living God.

Eli watched her mouth. Hannah spoke only in her heart, but her lips moved, trembling, quivering, murmuring, they moved but the sound of her voice was not heard.

Eli thought she was drunken. Eli spoke to her, "How long have you been like this? Put away the wine that clings to you."

Hannah answered him saying, "No, my sir, I am a woman of fierce spirit. I have neither wine nor strong drink to drink. I pour out my soul before the Living God. Do not regard your servant like a worthless woman because from out of a thousand thoughts and grievings, I have just poured forth my tumultuous words."

Eli answered her, saying, "Peace. Go in Peace. May the God of Israel give you that which you have begged to borrow from heaven." Hannah replied, "May your servant be full of grace in your eyes."

She went out. The woman went according to her own way and she ate. She no longer had a face of grief. She had a new face.

Her family rose up early in the morning, worshiped before God, and returned to their house in Ramah. There Elkanah made love with Hannah his wife and the Living God remembered her. In the natural coming round of days, Hannah conceived and she gave birth to a son. She named him Samuel, "Name of God," because from the Living God she had borrowed him.

Now the man Elkanah went up with all his household to offer their regular offering to God, their promised gifts. But Hannah did not go up. She said to her husband, "My gift is the lad and he is yet to be completed. I will bring him forth to be seen before God in due season. At that time he will remain, lent to God as a dedicated one forever."

Elkanah, her husband, said to her, "Do what is good in your eyes. Stay until you have completed him. Surely the Living God will maintain his counsel."

The woman settled down there. She fed her child, nourishing him on abundance and wisdom. Like a vinedresser she tended the youngster, training him up in the way he should go. He grew before her like a tender stalk.

When he was grown she took him up. With three oxen, one measure of grain, and a wineskin of wine, she came bringing him up to the house of the Living God at Shiloh and the lad was vigorous, a full, wholesome lad, complete in every way.

She worshiped, offering one of the beasts, then came to Eli with the lad Samuel, saying, "I entreat you, my sir. As surely as your soul is alive, I am the woman who was united with you in praying to the Living God for this lad here. I prayed and the Living God gave to me that which I begged to borrow from heaven. Now I lend him to the Living God. All the days which he lives he shall be borrowed from me by the Living God."

The lad bowed down, humbly, bending to the Living God. Hannah stood, mighty in Shiloh, proclaiming her prayer.

"My heart triumphs in the Living God.
My horn of strength rises, surging and exalted,
    like a silver temple trumpet lifted high and sounding,
    like a wild one's tusk, proud and tossing free,
    like a patriarch's shield, protecting and proclaiming
    God's standard to the nations
like the solitary mountain, high and isolate,
    from which the watcher's witness,
like the hand-hold hewn in the altar stone,

once grasped, supports the fallen,
like the fertile shoot, thrusting prophets and praisers
deep into generations to come,
like the radiant horns of light streaming from
the head of Moses.
My horn of strength streams forth praise
in the midst of the Living God,
surpassing all who plan evil against me.
My mouth opens wide, unafraid.
I rejoice in my Redeemer.
There is no one holy like the Living God,
like no other garment, our shade and our tent,
God is our clothing, our comfort,
like no other enclosure, refuge secure,
God is our rock and our mountain.
We are image and likeness of no other form,
God's icons living alive.
God is power! God is life!
There is no other one like our God.
God, you are fruitful, ever increasing,
your word soars, flying aloft, going forth freely.
You move mountains.
Stories about you pour forth from our mouths.
God who knows all things speaks, saying,
"I am the one who makes things happen."
By you alone are the gleanings measured.
Those who lay snares become shattered heroes,
the vulnerable you clothe in strength.
Those abundant in bread, have their own reward,
the hungry you yourself feed to fatness.
Even the childless gives birth to a throng
while the prolific weaken.

The Living God causes death and causes life,
    leads us down into hell and out again.
The Living God transforms existence, alters our substance,
    changes our mind,
    causing kinfolk and common ground,
    causing solitude and lowliness.
Yes, how much more does God cause us to grow,
    to rise up and redeem!
Thus the poor are raised up from the dirt,
    the troubled lifted from ashes.
They are set down in the care of those who are noble.
They even inherit a glorious seat of distinction, raised up
    like brides joyfully adorned,
    like queens splendid with honor,
    like high priests clothed in dignity.
All this is true. The Living God owns the stream of justice.

"Hell's watercourse is beneath the earth, the primal chaotic fertile waters contained by the Awesome One before time began. In the narrow deep is a swift running current swirling under the dust from which the surge welled up in Eden. Here on the rock by the riverside God mixed dust and blew into the nostrils of humankind the rush of life and they became alive.

"And it is here by the riverside that the watch of justice is set. God will guard the steps of those who have cared. People of kindness shall not slip into the whirlpool, neither shall they stumble off the brink. But the careless ones, the people who forgot, those who said they didn't know the difference between good and evil, they will be astounded by obscurity, numbed in confusion, silenced in gloom, and borne away in the flood-tide.

"Here by the riverside, those who cause justice, the Kind Ones, those whose name, like God's, is Compassion, will be anointed, their returning dust stirred, mixed again with the wellspring as in the beginning, formed anew by the Careful Crafter, lifted up like an offering, acceptable before the throne of God.

"It is not in human strength that we become winners victorious. The Living God shatters the striver, dismays the clamorer, and breaks down the fault-finder.

"The Most High God from the heavens, thunders.
　　　The one who causes all things to happen, reigns supreme
　　　　　from the beginning until eternity.
My God, you grant firm strength to those governors you designate.
You lift up high the horn of the redeemers you anoint."

Hannah's prayer was complete. She moved off toward the high places. Samuel, the lad, became "one who serves the Living God," ministering close by Eli, the priest.

Samuel served before the presence of the Living God, a lad girded in a white linen ephod worn over a long priestly garment, small, of a size for a lad. These things his mother made for him, bringing them up from season to season, at the set times she came with her husband to offer.

Eli blessed Elkanah, "one who is owned by God," and he blessed Hannah saying, "May the Living God place in your care a seed from this woman to replace the loan-child which she has lent to the Living God."

It came to pass that she conceived several times, giving birth to three sons and two daughters, and Samuel grew strong with the Living God.

Now Eli's sons were worthless men. They did not know God and their sin was great before God. People told tales of their travesty. The sons of Eli tormented worshipers, pressing their priestly privilege beyond its bounds, even raping the women who served at the very entrance to the Tent of Meeting. Eli admonished them for their violence saying, "I hear of your evil from the people."

But the lad Samuel moved on, growing continually, and he was good with the Living God and good with the people.

This is the story of Hannah. Her prophecy lives in every age of Israel. We hear her words in the mouth of Isaiah:

"Woe to those who regard not the work of the Living God,
    neither consider the labor of God's strength.
    Hell shall enlarge itself, opening its mouth without measure.
Woe to them that call evil good and good evil."

Hannah's voice is heard across the ages and her wisdom lives on in our prayer.

"People who do not measure their children by God's measuring rod, do not truly embrace them. Those who love their children teach them, correcting them when they are young. Even a child is known by his doings, whether her work is pure, whether it is right. The wisdom of women builds up wisdom's house.

"There are some who pretend to be rich yet have nothing. There are some who pretend to be poor yet have riches. Riches are ransom, the poor feel no threats.

"Wealth gotten by vanity is diminishing, wealth gotten by honest labor shall increase. Hope deferred makes the heart sick, desire fulfilled is a tree of life. Yes, those who oppress the poor blaspheme their Maker. Those who give graciously to the poor make a loan to the Living God. That which has been lent will be repaid."

From Hannah Israel learned to pray. Look around you. Where is your household in need of correction? Delve into your soul. Call forth your own strength. Mourn that which is not as it is intended to be. Grieve and weep. Feel the hand of God strong upon your shoulder. Stand fierce of spirit before the Living God, your rock and your redeemer, pouring out your soul like water, murmuring mightily,

today, tomorrow, day after day,
evening, morning, afternoon,
on your bed, at your table, in your garden.
As you journey on the way
become a murmurer of prayers,
become a vower and fulfiller of vows,
become one of the redeeming people.

THE STORY OF THE MOTHER OF SORROWS
Theologian of Resurrection

(1 Maccabees 1, 18; 2 Maccabees 6–7)

Miryam speaks:
Some of you call me "Mother of Sorrows."
    It is true, I have known great sorrow.
I stand now where she once stood.
      Near our home in Galilee, in a village square,
      a mother like me, with sons like mine
      was ravaged by Israel's enemies.
Let me tell you her story as it was told to me,
    a story I often told my son,
    a story we read from the later texts
        at the Feast of Lights in the winter.
Listen well to the tale of the Mother of Sorrows.

Three hundred years ago Alexander emerged from Macedonia. His armies coursing forth in all directions slaughtered, plundered, laid waste all the known nations, even the far-flung settlements. Twelve years he flaunted his prowess over a prone and quivering world, creating nations according to his own image. He swelled up with pride, then sickened. Dying, he divided his world twelve ways. His commandant-kings and their descendants continued their travesty upon us all. Our lot fell in the lap of the tyrant clan of the Syrian Antiochus, and Israel lived in a reign of awesome terror.

The Syrian published abroad to the nations, saying, "We will break Israel. Blot out all trace of her from the earth."

Each Jewish leader and priest in turn was offered the title "friend of the king" as a purchase price for their integrity. Some succumbed, saved their lives, and became courtiers and mock-celebrants. Some held fast to the teachings of Moses.

Sabbath observance was prohibited, women executed for kindling Sabbath lamps, men cut down with their babes in their arms as they lifted the Sabbath cup. Many fled to the caves in the hills and holed up there, hoping to escape, but they were betrayed, pursued, and burned alive in their hiding place. Their ashes drifted over the Land.

A just and beloved High Priest was murdered.

The Temple was pillaged and profaned. Screams of half-slain swine penetrated its sacred precincts. The agonized beasts careened through the holy sanctuary, flinging afar their pulsing blood to spatter remote silent spaces, which until that time had known only sweet herbal incense and prayer. Our prophets and singers were raped and ravaged in the gore as pagan priests sang and applauded.

So it was also in the villages. Altars for offerings of grain and oil and wine bore the stain and the smell of roasted pig. The stench of it filled our homes. Our sacred Torah scrolls were heaped upon the bloody pyres.

Month upon month, the campaign continued. Our sacred language was forbidden. Even under torture, should an old woman burst forth in prayer, public execution followed. Mothers who dared to defy the ban on circumcision had their eight-day infants hung to the death about their necks as they were paraded naked, flogged, spat upon and defiled, driven to their deaths. Yet, Israel found strength to resist.

It became the custom of Antiochus to create a great spectacle on our holy days. Jews were commanded to bear witness at the Temple stairs as our leaders were put to the test.

There was Eleazar, one of the leading teachers of the Torah, a man of great age and distinguished bearing. He was being forced to open his mouth and eat pig. He spat it out. The officials in charge of staging the sacrilegious feast urged him to prepare meat according to Moses' teachings, bring it to the sham celebration, and eat it in public, pretending it was their pig, and thus avoid persecution. He refused this deceit lest he lead astray the young and the doubting who might believe him a betrayer. He died a brutal public death nobly, standing in awe of the Living God, inspiring not only the young but the whole body of the nation.

So it was at just such a staged spectacle that our story takes place. The text relates:

"Among all our sages and leaders of that terrible time, the mother was the most remarkable of all and deserves to be remembered with special honor. Seven sons she had borne and raised up in the Way of God, the eldest a much-admired citizen, the youngest still held by the hand."

Antiochus ordered his henchmen to round up this respected family as the feature of his grim pagan circus. The mother he put on public display, her sons stood at her side.

Through the course of that terrible day, one by one the sons were put to the test. The faithful of Israel were rounded up and forced to watch. Antiochus presided. This mother — tradition names her both Miryam and Hannah — stood the day long, held up before the witnesses of Israel. Antiochus had his pagan priests sacrifice a pig to an idol, they feasted, gluttonous for the roasted flesh, and they brought portions, taunting, to force upon these Jews. One by one they died in tortured refusal.

They did not die silently, but preached and taught through the course of the entire tragedy. She encouraged them with her own teaching, speaking loudly in the forbidden Hebrew.

Finally, it was the turn of the last child, the little one she held by the hand. He too refused the pig thrust in his face on the tip of a sword. Antiochus begged the mother to convince her son. His planned festival was turning awry. Ablaze with spirit and wisdom, she spoke out these words to him, in the sacred tongue of the Jews, which witnesses recorded:

"My son, you appeared in my womb, I know not how. It was not I who gave you life and breath, who set your bones in order within your frame or knit your sinews. Our loving Creator formed you at your birth and knows who you are meant to be. Therefore, our loving Creator will give you back life and breath again, because now you put our holy way of life above all other thoughts."

The Syrian could not comprehend the language, but suspected that she was contemptuous of him. Antiochus appealed directly to the child, offering sweet enticements, assuring him on oath that the moment he abandoned his ancestral customs he would make him rich, enroll him as a "friend of the king," give him great and wondrous privileges. The child ignored him.

The king called out to the mother. "You speak to him. Urge your little lad to save his life."

Drawing the child away from the king, she bent toward him and spoke in the Jewish language,

"My beloved son, take my words to heart. I carried you within my womb for nine months. For three years fed you at my breast. Day after day I have taught you, raising you up to this very moment today. I invite you, my child, look all around you, up toward the sky, out over the hills, to the sea, down toward the earth. See all the wonder that is in them and understand that God made them all, everything out of nothing. People come into being the same way. Do not fear this butcher. Death too is from God. Accept it. You are worthy as your brothers are worthy. By God's love we will receive one another again when this day is completed."

Scarcely had she finished when the lad turned to Antiochus and his priests:

"Why do you delay? I do not attend to the laws of kings. I attend only to the Way given by Moses to our ancestors. And you who devise harm for the Hebrews, you will not escape God's hand. We sin and we are corrected and reconciled with the Living God, but you who harm God's servants are lost. God gave me my body and I return it to God gratefully. Pain is brief. God's promise is everlasting life."

His torture was the most brutal of all. He died trusting in God, perfect, pure, and sinless.

After her sons, the mother died also.

The king was beside himself with rage.

All these things led us to the terrible truth of those days. There is a time for peace and a time for war. This was a time for war. Judah Maccabee and his companions rose up. They made their way out of the wilderness into the villages unobserved. Led by God, they recovered the Temple and the city of Jerusalem. Together with the people they purified the Temple grounds, constructing a new altar. For the first time in two years the incense, the lights, and the bread of presence graced the place of sacred gathering. The joyful celebration lasted for eight days. Where only a brief time before they were hiding like wild creatures in the mountains, now musicians played, dancers danced, and garlanded singers chanted our ancient hymns to the One who had sustained them to this day. Yet, it would be another twenty years of struggle and war before the Syrians were driven from the last frontier of Israel's soil. The mother and her seven sons are buried on the hillside of Safed.

Israel remembers the Mother of Sorrows. We tell her story at the Feast of Lights in winter and we honor all who, like her, have held to the teachings of Moses.

The Mother of Sorrows leaves us with questions. Can one woman stand, watching the death of a son for the sake of God's teachings? Can one woman perceive the power of God and teach others to trust it beyond the grave? Can one woman bind her children to Torah and ask them to choose pain and death to sustain the way of our covenant?

Can one woman stand alone at any point in time and inspire a nation to exchange a brokered, bitter truce for the agony of battle? Can she declare with the prophet, "Peace, you say peace! There is no peace!"

Wisdom speaks:
"My Torah of Wisdom is a fountain of life,
    road departing from the snares of death.
"Mother, cherish your children. Rear them joyfully as a dove rears her nestlings. Teach them to walk without stumbling. 'You are my chosen,' says the Living God, 'I will raise up the dead from their resting place and bring them out of their tombs, for I have acknowledged that they bear my name. Have no fear, mother of many sons and daughters. I have chosen you,' says the Living God. 'Teach them that I bent the sky, shook the universe, spun the round world into its order. Teach them that the Living God makes the depths to shudder.'"

O understanding, be not hidden!
O reason, do not withdraw into your secret chamber!
    Make visible the shape of your voice.

THE STORY OF QUEEN SHALOM-ZION
Queen of Peace, City of Refuge

(From the historic records of Greece, Egypt, and Israel)

Miryam speaks:
Some of you call me "Queen of Peace,"
      some of you call me "City of Refuge."
  It is true, I am your leader.
      I am responsible for you before God.
      I seek to shape you as I shaped my son,
         as a people strong enough
            to secure the peace of many.
I stand now where our queen once stood.
Let me tell you her story as it was told to me,
  a story I often told my son,
  a story we read from the Scroll of Records.
Listen well to the story of Queen Shalom-Zion
      in whose hands all ages will declare was secured
         the Golden Years of Israel.

    Queen Shalom-Zion reigned in the days when my grandmothers lived, in my mother's childhood and in the childhood of the saintly Elizabeth, my kinswoman, with whom I have shared much.

Israel was complete. Her secure borders stretched from Dan to Beersheba, from Egypt to the Carmel, from the plains and cities well beyond the Jordan River through the hills of Galilee stretching to the sea.

Within our land the world knew us as a people of good heart, loving the way of our God and living with care. These days were the fulfillment of struggle. Before we proceed, we must know what came before.

On the 25th day of Kislev, a hundred years before her reign, Judah Maccabee, son of Mattathias, her kinsman, recaptured the Temple from Syrian-Hellenist forces. They shut down the Game of Kings in Israel. What had begun in humiliation ended in glory.

Sons and daughters of Aaron came from throughout the land to purify the Temple grounds on Mount Moriah. Scrubbing the stone pavements, we washed away the blood of swine, which sadistic armies had mixed with the blood of our children and sages.

Restoring the gates and the balustrades, we set stone next to stone together, repeating the pattern of Solomon's builders, repeating the work of the daughters and sons of Ezra's day.

Then, like them, we began eight days of purifying the Temple so that we might come before God on the eighth day, like a newborn child in the company of our ancestors, to renew our ancient covenant. We came in the spirit of our prophets inscribing our teachings upon our lives in a circumcision of our hearts. And God accepted our service, gifting us with wonders and miracles.

We danced our psalms, defiant and joyful, our feet pounding them into the pavement stone. Cymbal and harp, timbrel and voices, trumpet and shofar, our ancient horn, were lifted up high sounding forth from Mount Zion, ringing through the Judean hills. Thus Israel reclaimed her home.

Today we celebrate that Feast of Rededication. We call it the Feast of Lights in winter. Today Herod the evil Idumean reigns, married to Miriamne, Queen Shalom-Zion's granddaughter. Herod says this marriage aligns him with the great Hashmonean house. Our sages say Miriamne is like a precious ring of pure gold stuck in the snout of a pig.

Herod expanded the Temple grounds, creating a work of his grand design, a wonder of the world, they say. Even though today Romans strut through our nation, playing treacherously with us, causing some of our leaders to compromise for survival, still the Temple is our precious place of heritage. We have maintained the sacred precincts, and Rome has acquiesced to our fierce desire to keep the Temple pure. We still pray there every day. We dance and covenant our children as in days of old. We still celebrate the Feast of Rededication and will do so till the end of time.

Shalom-Zion's kin, the Maccabeans, led our state, creating the reign of the Hashmonean clan. When Jerusalem, our heart, was secure, they went out, whole families armed with ingenuity and heritage, responding to the Maccabees' cry, "Follow me!" One brother led until he was struck down. Upon his death another rose up. And so they went, each one keeping the Temple worship constant and the lands in till and harvest, while at the same time pushing back the hostile line.

For twenty years the cry of our enemies rang from the hills and echoed through the world: "Erase the name of Israel from the face of the earth, blot out her memory from the records of nations, drive her into the sea."

Twenty years we labored, prising loose the sacred land from the vise of Gentiles, throwing off the Syrian yoke. Twenty years before our people began again to write their own contracts and agreements dating them: "In the first year of Simon Maccabee, great High Priest, general, leader among the Jews."

The people were prepared for peace. As long as Simon Maccabee lived, the Record Scrolls say, he reigned over our nation in peace. He promoted people's welfare and they lived happily through the days of his reign. Simon secured our seaports again and continued pressing the borders. He was a righteous master, known in the world like Abraham. He returned prisoners, took no booty, brought our prisoners home, freed hostages, took no bribes. Each holy place he liberated was rededicated and made safe for prayer.

People farmed their land in peace and the land responded, producing crops in the hills. On the plains the trees fruited. Elders sat in the streets, talking together of their blessings. Simon saw that the abundance was distributed and all were secure from bandits. His renown reached the ends of the earth. He restored peace to the land and there was rejoicing throughout Israel. All sat under their own vines and fig trees, and they had no one to fear. The enemy vanished from the land. Simon gave protection to the poor and the stranger, paid attention to the teachers and rid the country of lawlessness. In this way he gave new splendor to the Temple.

Each Maccabean kin to follow assumed the mantle of Monarch-High Priest, striving to maintain the delicate balance between integrity and security.

But Israel's peace brought her abundance, and alien forces lurking at her borders lusted to pluck her fruit for themselves, to sip her fine wines at their banquets, to swath their bodies with the oil of her olives and to bathe in her milk and honey. She took on the appearance of a simple, naive population. A vulnerable lamb in the midst of wolves, grazing in her God-promised green pasture, beside still running waters, her only fence the Torah.

Meanwhile, we were also assaulted from within. The sweet seduction of Greece and Rome tempted many. There arose from among us passionate leaders, each with a way we might meet the world hammering at our gates, a world leaking through the mountain passes, filtering through the marketplace. A world flamboyant as legionnaires' plumes, thrilling to the stadium roar, succumbing to odors seductive. Unguents disguised the rot that was Rome, hid a world twisted in on itself with amusements, which our covenant with God kept us from playing.

In due time came the turn of the Hashmonean King Alexander Yannai. He was assailed from within and without by parties of sages, each certain that theirs was the only way to keep out the alien forces, to survive — simply to survive — in a world gone mad for Western power.

Shalom-Zion, Alexander's wife, was wise, astute in the ways of the world. Torah-true, she was loved by the people. She advised him but he ignored her counsel.

Alexander Yannai chose the party of the Sadducees. He chose to empower the few, an elite at ease with the ways of nations, conversant with courtiers, people of intellect, wealth, and grandeur. The Sadducees established a clerical caste which would stand between the world and the people as a barrier, a buffer not a bridge. At the same time, they demanded from the people ritual rigidity. "To make you strong," they said, "impenetrable." Alexander chose a party willing to negotiate with the lurking foe, to compromise with decadence. The Sadducees traded with tyrants. They played the Game of Kings, explaining away the betrayal by saying, "Is it not better for one to die for us all than for many to die for one?" Their stronghold was the Temple, their mandate a House of Lords.

Alexander Yannai rejected the party of the Pharisees. He rejected the policies of those who sought to empower the people. The Pharisees taught Torah to everyone. They declared that every observant believer was priestly, as proclaimed in the sacred text. This people's priesthood would stand as God stood, all-present in holiness everywhere. The Pharisees worshiped no earthly king. They committed themselves to the one and only governor of Israel, the Living God, in whom there is everlasting life. These teachers saw their stronghold as the synagogue, their mandate a court of justice called the Sanhedrin.

The Pharisees were put down, imprisoned, exiled, driven into desert caves. Those who persisted were executed in great numbers. A Greek advisor to the king, Diogenes by name, persuaded him to show the nations he was really in charge and instigated the crucifixion of eight hundred Pharisees.

When, after years of this rule, Alexander Yannai failed, Queen Shalom-Zion rose up to succeed him. The queen made her own choices and changed forever the course of Israel. One report says, "She was a strong leader, showing no signs of weakness, wise to the greatest degree. Ambitious in governing Israel, she demonstrated by her doings that she was fit for action."

She reigned nine years until her death at age seventy-three. She placed the Pharisees in authority, giving the Sadducees refuge in several walled cities not strategic to Judah's safety. She established trade and diplomacy throughout the known world, increased her armies to such a degree that all Israel's borders were strongly defended, becoming formidable to tyrants surrounding our Land. The country was entirely at peace. When the marauding generals of Armenia stormed through Syria, then ruled by Egypt, gathering a force to attack us, she alerted her embassies in Egypt, appealing directly to Queen Cleopatra, who called them off. An old alliance between the two monarchs turned back the threat to our frontiers.

The queen's name was known throughout the Gentile world as Queen Alexandra Salome, Sovereign of Israel. "The confidence of nations reposed in her. She succeeded in quieting the vexing internal dissension of the state, a result of Alexander Yannai's errors, without detriment to the political relations of the Jewish state in the outside world."

The queen made her own choices. She was a devout Jew. She rose up early each morning to pray the blessings, "because," she said, "the first breath of the day belongs to God, like the dew." Then, washing her hands and her eyes in pure water, blessing again, she made herself ready to stand before God alone. She tarried in silence one hour after the manner of the strong, then her voice could be heard in song, "Hear, O Israel, the Living God is your God, your only God."

She assembled her court each morning and evening, reading to them from the Torah scrolls leading the prayer, "because," she said, "our delight is in the Torah of God and upon it we will ponder both day and night."

She was an observant Jew and her brother was Simeon ben Shetah, the great Pharisee. During the reign of rage before her reign of peace, she arranged refuge for him and many others with Cleopatra in Egypt. When she assumed the throne, he returned.

Her son Johannan was a quiet man, unenthralled with political life, a man of spiritual ways and devout practices. Johannan she appointed High Priest. He too was loved and the people cast a coin in his honor calling him "Friend of all Jews."

Queen Shalom-Zion set in place a familial leadership — mother, brother, son . . . monarch, sage, High Priest — according to the Torah tradition of Israel.

The queen's name was known throughout the Jewish world, from Babylon to Rome, from Elephantine and Alexandria to the land of cedars northward, "Queen Shalom-Zion, Malkah Israel" — Queen of Peace, City of Refuge, Lion of Judah, Monarch of Israel. The confidence of the Hebrew people rested upon her. Indeed, even King Alexander realized her worth at his dying. He proclaimed from his deathbed to all those standing by that she alone — not his sons, not with advisors — but she alone must succeed him, "because the Jews will follow her authority as they will no other." Events had revealed the wisdom of her advice and she had won the affection and respect of her people.

Truly, Jerusalem and all of Israel was secure in her hands. Her ambassadors, merchants, and scholars were welcome everywhere. She freed political prisoners, opened the borders to refugees, ransomed our hostages from Greece and Rome, signaled the exiles to safety. Jews returned from all the known world, and those who remained in their distant homes renewed their faithfulness and came up on pilgrimage at the great seasons of religious festival. The Pharisees built up the nation within.

Simeon ben Shetah established schools throughout Israel, sending teachers into the hills and lifting up the people of the land with learning. Synagogues were built everywhere and in great numbers.

The queen reorganized the Sanhedrin as a full representative body to act for justice, setting in force again the ways of Ezra. She reestablished the marriage contract, strengthening this legal writing so that no woman with children would ever be left destitute either by fate or faithlessness.

Her sagacity and tact succeeded in accomplishing security and integrity where all the martial force of her husband failed. She was seen as a sage, and the people loved her. As Alexander had foreseen, the people responded to her command, "Follow me." She revived the teachings of Ezra. Men, women, and children of the age of understanding came regularly to the Temple with gifts of gratitude. Women, men, and children of the age of understanding read from the Torah scrolls in the synagogues and taught the teachings to others. Children of the age of understanding, women, and men paused in the midst of their working days for prayer — lifting their mantles to cover their head. Entering the "tent of meeting God," some wearing phylacteries pressing the seal of God's word on their hearts and minds, binding their arms like a sacrifice lifted up to the altar of God, they prayed just as I do today. They prayed Hannah's great pouring out of the soul, just as I teach you to do.

Many came from other lands just to live the seven years of a Nazarite vow, for the vow can only be lived in Jerusalem, and they returned to their distant communities rededicated to teachings of kindness.

When the time of her dying came, Queen Shalom-Zion gathered her Elders, her priests, and her counselors before her. She said:

"I will not proclaim a successor. I have lived my life according to the teachings of the Living God as handed down to us by Moses. I have lifted up with my life God's wondrous name in praise and thanksgiving. God's strong arm has encompassed me about and I have been faithful. All generations will remember me and call me blessed.

"The people of Israel have become a great people. We have established peace. Even as we speak conquerors hover both within and without the Land, awaiting my death. My teachers, my priests, my people, I give the monarchy to you. I return rule directly into your hands. As in the days of the prophet Hannah's son Samuel, I return you to the reign of the Living God. Do whatever you deem righteous. I am able only to order my own actions while I am alive. I cannot secure your future from beyond the grave.

"You have many circumstances in your favor. The people are in good heart, the army is strong, you have money in all your treasuries.

"I have finished. It is completed. I render my reign into God's hands and yours. I accept the gift of death expecting the survival of my soul, the revival of my body. I expect to appear for judgment, accountable for my days before the Awesome One, our God of compassion. I expect to be reunited with you all in the life of the world to come. Blessed be the name of the Living God."

Once more she sang her evensong, "Hear, Israel, the Living God is your God, your only God." And she gave herself up to dying.

This is the story of Queen Shalom-Zion, who we call Queen of Peace and City of Refuge.

The sages record many remembrances from the golden years of her reign. They say that during these years heaven and earth bore witness to her righteousness.

Heaven, they say, witnessed her goodness. For seven years, no rain fell except on the Sabbath and every Sabbath the heavens poured forth their healing rain. Therefore, the poor never lost an hour's working wage, and even the stranger among us enjoyed a complete day of rest. The heavens provided the Sabbath. This testimony is written in the Temple scroll, for we have kept the evidence so that all future generations may witness, may know and understand that heaven responds to righteous living.

Earth, they say, witnessed her goodness. For seven years the earth blossomed unusually in our hands. During her reign the Land of Israel was so fertile that the grains of wheat, oats, and lentil grew to remarkable size and we can see the evidence ourselves in the Temple schools, for they have kept baskets of them for future generations to witness, to know and understand that the earth responds to righteous living.

We learned in the reign of Queen Shalom-Zion that the Day of the Messiah is indeed possible on this earth, in our days and in our lifetimes.

When those who are "fair to look upon" rule, when God's own governors come into power, then there is peace.

Wisdom speaks:

"The Living God keeps watch over all of you, a faithful lover, a strong shield and a firm support, a shelter from the scorching wind and midday heat, a safeguard against stumbling and falls. God raises your spirits and makes your eyes sparkle, giving health and life and blessing. The spirit of living souls is the lamp of the Living God, searching out their inmost parts.

"Kindness and truth preserve God's governor. Her throne is held up by fidelity. Like a fresh running stream, a mighty watercourse, is the monarch's heart in the hand of the Living God, directed as God chooses.

"One who honors God is gracious to the poor.

"Righteousness exalts a nation, but carelessness is shame.

"By fidelity and truth is iniquity purged. By fear of the Living God, we depart from evil. When our ways are pleasing to God, even our enemies take notice.

"O monarch, O sovereign of the nation, open your mouth and speak! Speak for those who cannot speak for themselves. Uphold the cause of all who are condemned. Speak up, judge righteously with kindness, plead the cause of the poor and the needy. Cut a swath between lives cramped and tedious and lives spacious with meaning. Deliver your people from the narrow places. The Garden of Eden lies open to you. The Tree of Life is planted and fruited, the coming age is ready, abundance safely stored. The city is built. Rest from fruitless toil is assured. The work of righteousness awaits you. Goodness and wisdom are brought to perfection."

Part Two: Prayer

As we begin our praise, petition, and thanksgiving, we say:

"O Living God,

    open my mouth

       and my lips will pour forth

         your hallelujahs."

When we come to the end of our prayer, let us say:
"May the words of my mouth and the meditation of my heart
be always acceptable in thy sight."

These are the prayers we pray, after the manner of the prophet
Hannah...

Magnificat of Ancestors

Remember, my soul,
    yours is the God who remembers.
Remember, my spirit,
    yours is the God who beckons,
    beckons both the willing and the unwilling,
        summons some among us to a special servitude.
My God, our God,
    from generation to generation you hover over your creation,
    Wise Witness, Mighty Challenge, Blessed Assurance.
    You speak and we respond.
And therefore you became
    God of Abraham and Sarah,
    God of Isaac and Rebecca,
    God of Jacob and Leah and Rachel,
    God of each and all our ancestors.
Then you called my name.
    I heard you and I answered.
Now I too stand among the summoned.
    Take me.
    Let me set your sacred seal upon my heart.
    I will cherish it as my shield forever.

You alone are the Holy One.
Your surging power fills the firmament.
Your sweet promises defy reason,
    simply your presence sets me on fire,

my heart pounding within me,
my blood coursing like a frightened deer.
You are the Generous One,
who shaped your creatures with kindness.
We belong to you because you love us.
The mistakes that we make in our lifetime
cast a stained shadow all about us,
they haunt us all our days.
Yes, our errors live three, even four generations.
However, because of you,
the good that we do creates light in the world,
living on even into the thousandth generation.
Because Abraham followed you, leaving kin and security,
I too can follow you.
Because Abraham obeyed you, trusting even beyond understanding,
I too trust you.
Because Sarah laughed in your wonderful miracles,
I too can delight and rejoice in your mysteries.
Because Sarah made an agonizing choice for you,
I too can make the choices that tear at my heart.
Because our ancestors stood with you so faithfully,
a mighty house was raised up;
age after age we have served you here
and you have been with us.
Together we are a blessing in the Land.
Because they stood, there is a place for me to stand.
Because I stand here today, others will stand after me.
You are the Ancient and Future Rememberer,
making choices day to day,
our Sovereign, our Helpmate, our Savior, our Shield.
Today, I enter your house, putting you on as a garment.
You are our mantle, your emblem emblazons our actions.

You are our shield of identity, our fragile protection,
   our horn of praise raised up in song.
You are our ancient shield, treasure of Abraham and Sarah,
   ours forever and only today.
   May we pass it on in strength.
   May we never bring shame on your household.
   May earth, your beloved creation,
      thrive and rejoice in our care.
      May we build with you a kind and honorable tradition
      for tomorrow.

"Blessed are you, Shield of Abraham,
   who remembers the good that we do."

Magnificat of God's Power

Awake, my soul,
>   believe the saving power of God.

Awake, my spirit,
>   witness the awesome strength of God.

You, Living God, give life to the dead.
>   Only in your vitality are we redeemed.
>   Only in your life-force are we sustained.

You, who alone are powerful,
>   have done great things for us.

Your name is Holy Redeemer.

We have seen your loving wonders.

Age after age we behold your countless labors
>   on our behalf.
>   We are amazed, awe-struck, humbled, and trembling
>   in the presence of your power.

Where people are fallen, you help us lift them up.

Where people are sick and wounded, you teach us to heal them.

Where people are confined, you move us to free them.

Everywhere you are called Fulfiller of the Faithful,
>   for you alone keep faith with those asleep in the dust.

Who is like you, Source of Power? Who can compare?
>   You are the cause of life.
>   You are the cause of death.
>   You are the cause of resurrection.

You cause salvation to sprout forth from doom,
   the dead to live anew in your strength.

"Blessed are you, Redeemer,
   who brings forth life from death. Amen."

MAGNIFICAT OF HOLINESS

Bend, my soul, and bow.
Kneel, my spirit,
    lay face down upon the dust,
        for you are in the presence of the Living God,
           your hope and your Redeemer.

Tremble, my reason, and fear.
Break open, my heart,
    hold yourself ready for change,
    for you stand here and now before the Living God
        whose name is "I Love You Forever."
Ancient and eternal God,
From generation to generation, you are "El,"
    Holy Power, Awesome One.
    You have reigned over us because
        you alone truly care.
           You alone lift us up.

Holy, Holy, Holy Living God of witnesses,
    all creation is filled with your glory!

May our hallelujahs be heard ringing through time.
Holy are you, enthroned upon the praises of Israel.
Because our holy ancestors trusted you, we too trust you.
Because they sang their songs of your steadfast love,
    today we sing our praise.

Because they assure us that
    the world is built by love,
        your faithfulness established even in the heavens.
They say, and we know, that your forearm is mighty.
    Strong is your hand, your powerful right arm raises high.
Right actions and justice are the foundation stone
        of your seat of distinction.
Love and truth clear a pathway before you.
        The joy of lovers, yes, familial happiness with you,
          is the bread of all those who sing your melody.
We walk a road, Holy One, lit by your teachings.
In your name we rejoice all the day long.
Each hour of the day you fill with opportunities
    for us to reach out and be kind.

Holy, Holy, Holy, Living God Sabbaoth.
    Remembering you is holy.
    Choosing you an act divine.
        Accept us as we stand before you.
        Hear our prayer.

"Blessed are those who come bearing your name.
    Hoshana in the highest."

MAGNIFICAT OF RESPONSIBILITY

Pay attention, my spirit, and listen.
>   Pause! Wait! Hear the word of God.
Ask my soul, and receive.
>   Treasure up in your heart God's inheritance.
You, Maker-God, have endowed us with knowledge,
>   knit into our bones a passion for worship,
>   bred into our fiber a bent for your ways.
>   Cautiously curious, that's how you made us,
>>   then tempted us steadily, "Come, taste and see!"
Drawn in the indigo of antiquity,
>   seen in the amber of the first light,
>>   you fashioned us lovingly, built us for joy.
You are the Holy One,
>   we are your image.
>>   If we but murmur, you call us by name.
>>   If you but whisper, listening we hear you.
You, Maker-God, have made us for wisdom.
>   "Perfect," you said, "Be just like me.
>>   Ask and I'll teach you.
>>   Search and you'll find me."
>   These are your promises, how dare we doubt?
You, Maker-God, have made us for understanding.
You came to your servant Daniel, saying,
>   "Understand, O child of earth, understand."

You say to us, "Children, my children,
    if only you accept my teaching,
        treasuring up my instructions.
    If only you incline your ear to my wisdom,
        softening your heart, you will understand.
    Wisdom waits for you, hovering.
        Cry out for her, lift your voice in loud lament.
        Seek her like silver. Stalk her like gold.
        Plan for her day and night.
        Design the moments of your life expecting her presence.
        Store up common sense like a vast royal treasure."
You, Maker-God, have made us for discernment.
    In you we may choose to know what we know.
        Knowing, we enter authentic choosing,
            claiming your pathway, uniquely our own.
Your name is Risk, Terrible Daring.
    Hardy Adventure, I call you by name.
        You are Reality, Only Security.
    If you are my helper, how can I fall?
        Without you my soul dwells in numbness.
When I panic, "Ah, my foot slips!"
you say, "I will hold you."
When I murmur, "Oh, my cares are too many, too hard,"
    you say, "Here, find comfort in me."
When I complain, "Look at them all, gathering against me.
        Mischief they make, then frame it in laws,
        stupidity heaped up in my direction,
        nit-picking, faultfinding all the day long,"
    you say, "Patience. Let me defend you."
Truly, you are our rock and our refuge.
Truly, you help us make the road straight.

Generation after generation, you have assured us,
    "Ask and I'll teach you. Seek and you'll find."

"Blessed are you, Maker-God of all creation,
    who has endowed us with knowledge and wisdom,
        understanding and discernment."

MAGNIFICAT OF REPENTANCE

Come forth, my soul, have courage.
>   Bend low, my spirit, before your God.
>   Trust in the love that is offered.

Abba, bring us home to your teachings.
Sovereign, bring us near to serve at your right hand.

Turn us and we shall be turned.
Return us to yourself in perfect repentance.

Abba, remember what you have said,
>   "It's the charge of a father to teach his child.
>   Can a mother forget the babe at her breast?"
>   Kings don't forget their inheritors.

By you are all our actions weighed.
>   By you alone are our gleanings measured.
>   Accept our prayer of repentance.

You alone are the Holy One.
>   You alone forgive us and long for us to return.

Our Father, our Father, we come.
>   Mother us now as in days of old.
>   Care for us as you did East of Eden.

O Living God, great and faithful God,
      who keeps covenant and troth with those who love you,
            with those who keep your commandments.
      We have been careless . . .
            not once but again and again.
      We have left your teaching with intention and planning,
            rebelled, turned from your face,
                  and disclaimed you.
      We have become confused.
Incline your ear to us and hear us.
      Open your eyes and see us standing here.
We do not come to you because of our goodness,
      but because of yours.
O God hear! O God forgive! O God hearken to us
      and act quickly.

God who brought us out of the narrow place,
      we kneel before you, naming our failures,
      beating our breast, we give voice to our sins one by one.

In the midst of our error, we take heart from your words to the
prophet Daniel. You said to him, "I come to give you the skill of discernment and understanding. At the moment you began to form words
of confession, at the instant we heard your plea, the commandment
went out. I come to tell you, 'Know this, my child, and understand, you
are the greatly beloved.'"

"Blessed are you, Faithful Father, Mother of All Creation,
      who welcomes the words of the penitent."

MAGNIFICAT OF FORGIVENESS

Abba, forgive us,
    because we have sinned against you.
        Relinquish your right to punish us.
Abba, blot out our sins,
    because they have tarnished your name.
        Relinquish your right to remember them.

        Our guilt is evident in your eyes.
        Take it from us completely.
        Make it vanish from existence.

Abba, lift us up to the light, pure again,
    cleansed by your compassion,
        washed in your love,
            perfect and free as the day you made us.
Abba, forgive us and we shall be forgiven.

Your holiness saves us.
    We are here because you love us.
    We do your will because we love you.
    You forgive our carelessness when we admit it,
        erase the record of our rebellion when we return.
    You accept all the good that we do
        and redeem our life from the narrows.

Judge of the World, I can be re-formed in you.
    I forgive every evil, every wrong done to me.
        Let no one be punished on my account.
    Let my yes be yes, and my no be no.
        The sum of my gleanings generous.
I carry your Torah in the marrow of my bones
    and with your way I am enfleshed.
Your word courses in the pulsing of my blood
    and your presence is my nourishment.
In you I am poured out like water on parched earth.
In you I become an altar stone, a thirsting deer,
    bread for the world.

Lover of my soul, remember your promises
    made to us in the desert.
You said, "I come to redeem you because you cry out to me.
    Your cry is like thunder to my ears and I always hear you. I come
        because my name is Giver of Peace."

"Blessed are you Gracious Giver, Caretaker of the Universe,
    take note of your children standing before you,
        take note of us and forgive."

Magnificat of Redemption

Stand up, my soul,
    lift your eyes to the mountain.
        From the Rock, our God, will come your freedom.
Step forward, my spirit,
    dry your tears.
        It is time to claim your inheritance.

Holy One, look at us.
    See the repentant grieving before you.
    See the repairs we have made for our sins.
    See the resolve with which we are strengthened.

What is goodness? What do you require of us except that we
    "be like you in our judgment, love kindness and be modest before
        you"?
Take us up and redeem us quickly,
    for you desire not the death of sinners but that we return and live.
Who is like you? Surely there is no other.
    You refuse to be angry forever because compassion is your delight.
        In your mercy our wrongs are erased.

O Living God, unless you build our house, we labor in vain.
    Unless you keep our cities, the watchers we post are pretentious.
Those who trust in you are like Mount Zion,
    which cannot be moved but abides forever.

As the mountains are round about Jerusalem,
    so the Living God is round about us,
        now and forever surrounding.
When God brought us back from Babylon to Zion
    we were like people who dream,
        our mouths filled with laughter,
        our tongues singing songs.
    And the nations saw us saying to one another,
        "See what their God does for them!
        Their God redeems them from captivity!"
We were like water in the desert rushing free.
We who sowed in tears, reaped in joy.

Happy are we when our actions are blameless.
Happy are we when we walk toward God.
Happy are we when we return, keeping faith,
    wholeheartedly, diligently, not being ashamed.

"Blessed are you, our Only Redeemer."

Magnificat of Healing

Reach out, my soul,
    grasp the strength of God.
Touch it, my spirit, and be complete.
Heal us, Kind Healer, and we will be healed.
Restore us and we will be restored.

You are the Holy One,
    you know our needs.

When we murmur, you hear us.
When we cry out, you understand.

Who is like you, O Living Healer?
    There is no other.
        Only a fool says secretly, "There is no God."

Is anything too wonderful for you?
    Do not hide your face from us now, for we have trusted you.
    Repair us as you did in Eden, build us up into new forms.

We pray for ourselves,
    for our families and those we hold dear,
    for our neighbors and friends,
    for members of the community.
We pray for all people who pray to you.
    May their prayers be answered.

We pray for all people who cannot pray.
    Perceive their needs and answer them.

Mighty Restorer, be merciful,
    heal our souls.
Skillful Physician, be gracious,
    heal our bodies.
Eternal Presence, quiet those who are afraid.
Gentle Comforter, accompany those who mourn.

"Blessed are you, Healer, Deliverer, Sustainer, and Redeemer.
    We have nothing good apart from you.
    May it be your will
        to heal us with a perfect healing, body and soul,
        and to fill your people with life and peace."

Magnificat of Harmony

Tend the earth, my spirit.
Till the heavens, my soul.

Tenderly God endowed creation with blessing, saying,
  "You are to bear fruit, to be many and changing,
     complete the earth and fill it up.
  Inhabit my place, make it your home, govern it as I would.
  Make it my footstool, the place of my rest,
     my home, my very delight.
  Here it is! Take it, please, I give it all to you,
     every seed-bearing plant upon the face of the entire earth,
     every tree and its tree-fruit bearing seeds of its own kind.
  This is your food and the food of everything that lives,
     the flyers and swimmers, the crawlers and swarmers,
     the wild rovers, and the gentle herds.
  Amazing this is! Exceedingly wonderful.
  It is good to live, good to die, and good to continue
  forever, together."

Holy are you.
  Perfect is your creation.
  Your intention is toward prosperity.
Faithful are you, our Attentive Employer.
  You give us due reward for our labor.
     We reap what we have sown.

From generation to generation you reassure
    those who live in fear of you,
    those who live in holy awe, respecting your sacred power.
Those who violate the forces of life are confused.
    Works of arrogance rot in storage.
    Harvests of pride poison partakers.
    Fake abundance fills the belly, but fails to nourish.

Have you not said to us in the wilderness school,
    "If you hearken diligently to my teaching with which I
    instruct you in this day,
        to love the Living One, your God, and to serve with all
        your heart and with all your soul,
    then there shall be caused the giving forth of rain over
    your land, seasonal rains, the early rain to soften the
    ground for planting and the later rains to fill your
    cisterns before the summer dryness,
        in order that you may gather your grain, your fruit for
        wine, and your oil.
    I will cause the giving forth of grass that you may feed
    your cattle, nourishing them.
    Beware within yourselves. Let your hearts not become
    foolish. A satisfied appetite sometimes lulls the mind.
    Become not foolheardy, turning away from me.
        I am the life-force. When you serve other gods, even
        worshiping them, snubbing my power, I am enflamed
        against you. Heaven casts forth water no longer. The
        Land becomes lifeless. Those who turn the Land God
        gives them into a land of idolatry, perish.
    Therefore lay up my words within your hearts and deep within
    your souls. Bind them as a seal upon your hand and between
    your eyes, teaching them to your children, speaking about

them as you sit in your homes, as you walk here and there, when you lie down and when you rise up. Write these, my teachings, on your doorposts and your gates. In this way, many will be your days and your children's days in the Giving Land of my covenant. They shall be as the days of heaven upon the earth."

"Blessed are you, Living Creator, Tender of Heaven and Earth,
    who satisfies the faithful with goodness,
  who causes your divine presence to rest upon earth
    where the land is worked with integrity."

Magnificat of Ingathering Exiles

Listen, my soul,
    perhaps in our lifetime God's shofar will sound.
Keep watch, my spirit,
    soon the standard will rise,
    soon, the Day of the "Great Coming Home."

You are the Holy One,
    gather us round you.
        Summon the outcasts to enter within the gates.
        Inform the prisoners of their freedom.
        Invite the oppressed to their liberation.
        Signal the exiles to safety.

As for those clustered on the margins of our societies,
    those we assign to the fringes of our assemblies,
        it is our worldly systems that shove them aside.
        It is "efficiency," "economics," "political wisdom,"
            "porous piety," "the greater good,"
                and "majority rule."
        It is attitudes like "After all, what can we do?"
        or "See, they bring this on themselves."
        It is protection and preservation.
        It is fear that delegates some among us to be marginalized.
        It is not your desire.

O that we might discern between separation and condemnation.

O that we might discern between fences built
     high enough to insure our sacred uniqueness
     and low enough to share bread and justice.
O that we might discern between the stranger and the enemy.
     Is this not what you ask of us?

O God, we are a pregnant people, long in labor.
     Deliver us of this child
          and let her name be called Security.
O God, we are a laboring people, diligent in righteousness,
     bring forth your harvest
          and let her name be called Peace.
O God, we are a ready people, preparing your household as you
  have taught us.
     Gather your guests, begin the Great Festival,
     let her name be called Perfection.
          Have you not instructed us, saying,
               "Be you perfect even as I am"?

Let it not be said of us,
     "When I came looking for you, you were not there,
          calling you, you did not answer."
May all people form a single band
     to do your will with a perfect heart.

"Blessed are you, Living God, Householder of Heaven and Earth,
     who decides the perfect time,
     who will someday declare the great day of ingathering exiles."

Magnificat of Justice

Reveal yourself, my soul,
    let your deeds proclaim your identity.
Return yourself, my spirit,
    restore the validity of our ancient judges.

You alone, O God, in loving kindness and compassion,
    you alone try us, correct us, and clear us in judgment.
        You alone restore us clean and free in your care.

Holy are you. Lit clear is your pathway.
    From generation to generation
        we attend the prophet's clarion call,
        "Cease to do evil, learn to do good,
        seek judgment, lift up the pressed down,
        consider the homeless,
        plead for the woman abandoned, with child."

Hasten the time when no one will trample on the vulnerable,
    when wickedness will be wholly consumed in your selective fire,
    when the dominance of the arrogant will pass away.

O let us not become the oppressors.
    Let us not do harm to others,
        nor mar the face of your creation.
    Let us not stand idly by in the blood of our neighbors.

O save us from believing we understand everything.

Save us from age-old animosities and trivial solutions.
Save us from slogans and battle cries,
from dogma without dedication.
Sovereign of Justice,
kindle us with clarity, enlighten us
with memories of our own liberation.
We who are in power now, flawed by fame and fear,
help us see our twisted accusations of the other ones.
Enflame us with compassion,
fuse our lives with those whose lives are in bondage.
Refine our rage. Temper us into vessels useful and sound.
Etch upon us your design.
Help us to correct our own violences,
to fix what we have broken.
Help us to choose not to be stupid and naive.
Help us to forgive others when they have repented,
made repairs, and changed their actions.
Help us to remember what must be remembered
and forget what must be forgotten.
Help us to know the difference between them.

Then we can ask you to forgive us.
Then we may sow justice and reap mercy.
Then we may claim our promised destiny.
Then justice will roll down like water and
righteousness like a rushing river.

"Blessed are you, Holy Governor,
who values right actions and clear judgments,
who raised up Deborah and Solomon,
judges wise and mighty in days of old,
who will raise up judges wise and mighty again in our time."

Magnificat of Protection

Be watchful, my spirit.
>Separate from those who bring you down.

Take care, my soul.
>Refuse to be defined by raves and urges.

"Living God, who shall abide in your tent?
>Who shall dwell in your Holy Mountain?
>Only those who move cleanly,
>who act kindly,
>who speak truly in the depth of their hearts."

You, Holy One are our protection.
>We dwell among people wed to undermining ways.
>We dwell in the midst of seduction.
>We dwell among usurpers.
>>Betrayal is our bread.
>Protect us, Holy One, save us from temptation.

As your prophet Isaiah warned us,
>"Woe to them that bind iniquity to themselves like a bridle of vanity.
>Woe to them that drive sin as with the cords of a cart.
>They say, 'Quickly,' 'Make haste,'
>>'Look, we ourselves will push God's purposes nearer.
>>Come, see the Great Day.'
>Woe to them that call evil good and good evil.

Woe to them that are wise in their own eyes,
   that see common sense as their way alone."

As for those who slander us, let them not be encouraged.
   Confuse our enemies, confound their plans,
      scatter their efforts to destroy us.

"Blessed are you, our Creator, Protector of the Faithful,
   who scatters and confuses those who lessen your people, Israel."

Magnificat of Fidelity

Embrace, my soul,
    those who turn to God, wondering.
Companion, my spirit,
    those who are kind.

Age after age God summons witnesses.
Age after age people respond.
Age after age holiness seasons creation.

O God, you are that holiness,
    lifted up, exalted, and celebrated by those who love you.

You remember your saints and sages of old.
    The good they accomplished lives on.
You sustain your saints and sages alive in the world today,
    encouraging them, clearing their way.
You lift up those newly come to your teachings.
    Like newborn babes you cherish them softly.
    Clarify their plans, strengthen their efforts,
        deepen their commitment.
Let them soar as though they flew on the wings of an eagle.
Let them run swiftly and never grow weary.
Let them learn well and find friendship among us
    in order that they may walk the long walk
        and never grow faint.

Grant a good life to the true of heart.
    We cast our lot among them,
        let none of us be put to shame.

"Blessed are you, our God, Loving Companion,
    teacher of all you call to your side,
        who sustains and encourages good people."

Magnificat of Messianic Age

Come, my spirit,
    our people ask a favor of God.
Bow low, my soul,
    we voice our request.

Holy One of Israel,
    There once lived among us David, your anointed one.
    O God, cause his generations to flourish forth again.
    There once lived among us holy governors,
    servants appointed by you, just and redeeming.
    O God, bring forth their offspring to govern again.
    There have been times, many times,
        when peace and prosperity reigned,
        when Israel was a light to the nations,
        when we were a blessing to all the families of earth.
    Let that time come again.
    Let it be sustained and spread out over all creation.
    Let it be forever.

In that day when your anointed begins to reign,
    all earth shall be attentive.
    All people shall believe, whispering to one another,
    "Come neighbor, come friend, set down your burden.
    Strike no fire, mend no seam.
        The Great Sabbath has begun."

And in that great day,
    "You will give us shepherds after the ways of your own heart, who
    shall feed us knowledge and understanding.
    We will become many in that day, bringing the land to abundance
    and no one shall speak of the Ark of the Covenant, nor remember
    it, pining, nor miss it, because we will have learned and we will
    be living the Holy Teachings.
    In those days Jerusalem itself will be God's seat of distinction,
        all nations gathered close in her embrace,
            gathered to honor the name of God
                gathered here in Jerusalem.
And no one will move ever again
    to the command of the rigid and evil-hearted."

Holy One of Israel,
    favor us with peace,
    cause your Messiah to come,
    bring your reign to fullness.

"Blessed are you, Holy God, Sovereign of Heaven and Earth,
    who anoints shepherds of your own choosing
        and appoints them to govern in kindness."

Magnificat of Acceptance

Speak truthfully, my soul.
    Your God is listening.
    Let your words pour forth from your heart.
Know this, my spirit,
    the Living God is the one who hearkens to prayer,
        the only one who redeems us.

You are the God who listens to the prayers and pleas
    of this murmuring people.
You are the God who hears and responds.
You are holy. Compassionate Listener is your name.

Never say in your heart,
    "I am hidden from God."
Never tell yourself,
    "Who is there from so far off that pays attention to me?
    In such a crowd of humanity, no one will notice.
    I am but a blade of grass in the vast acreage of creation."
Know this, every particle in the heavens, in the great deep,
    in the earth, even in all the mountains and the valleys,
        resounds in response to God's presence.
        Each has a heart and that heart pulses to the glaze of
        God's glance.
Who among us can grasp such things?
Who can comprehend God's totality?
    There are those who say,

"Justice is difficult to understand.
Who can discover God's reasoning?
These teachings are obscure, remote from us,
     long ago and far away."
These are the fantasies of tiny minds,
     the absurdities of shallow spirits.
These are the idle daydreams of stupidity.

Living God who hears prayer,
     cause us to realize your will,
     cause us to come to your understanding, not our own.
There is much to which we are blind,
     many things which you alone see.
     Do what is good in your sight.
We come pleading, turn us not empty away.
We come longing, hide not your face from us.
We come humbly, accept our prayer.
Give to every person their daily bread.
Answer in your wisdom every heartfelt prayer.
Our needs before you are many, our knowledge slender.
Grant us goodness according to your will.

"Blessed are you, the Living God, Compassionate Presence,
     hovering throughout the universe,
          who sees us with understanding,
          who hears our prayers and responds,
          who grants goodness according to wisdom."

Magnificat of Joyful Service

Be glad, my soul.
    Go up to the Holy Mountain.
Be joyful, my spirit.
    Your service is required at a sacred table.
Make a joyful noise to God.
    Let all the earth join in with praise.
Make your hallelujahs echoes of gladness.
Sing psalms, pluck melodies, declare love poems and dance.
Let the roar of the sea accompany its crooning creatures,
    the thunder harmonize with a heavenly choir.
Let the river waves clap and the dust keep time.

We light lamps with holy olive oil,
    picked from the trees, pressed by our labor.
We knead bread with finest flour,
    reaped from the fields, milled by our work.
We pour wine of choice fruit,
    pulled from the vine, seasoned by our toil.
O Living God, accept in love and favor our offerings and prayer.
    Accept with delight our festive liturgy.

You are the Holy One. Humbly we serve you.
    Imprint us with awe for all your wonders.
    Impress us with respect for the work of your creation.
    Seal us with honor for the dignity of your teachings.

We are always in your presence,
> every place, every moment, near at your hand.
Accept our sacred celebrations,
> our Sabbaths and New Moons.
When we are deaf to your rustling Spirit,
> our feasts are empty displays.
When we ignore your righteous urging,
> our efforts are deceitful.
When we fail to secure justice and compassion,
> our liturgy grieves you.

We come today prepared.
> Our repentance and restitution rest at your feet.
We come in reverence as David once came,
> serving you with gladness,
> coming into your presence in song,
> knowing that you alone are God.
>> You made us. We belong to you.
>> We are your people, the sheep of your pasture.
Enter. Enter God's gates with thanksgiving.
> Enter God's courtyard with praise.
Be thankful, acknowledge God's blessings.
> God is good. Steadfast in loving, enduring forever,
>> faithful to all generations.

"Blessed are you, Holy One, our Maker and Shepherd,
> you alone do we follow.
> You alone do we serve.
> May our worship be always true,
>> our liturgy acceptable in your sight."

Magnificat of Gratitude

Count them, my spirit, and be grateful.
    Count the wonders one by one,
        each drop of rain, each kiss,
        each kindly word, each rose and garlic bud.
Observe them all, my soul, and give thanks.
    How many times have you been redeemed?
    How many breezes blew clouds away?
    How many seeds burst into life?
Holy is God, alive and active.
You, dear God, have loved us with a sweet and tender love.
    Like a Father you have corrected us,
        chastising us sorely as only a mother can.
When we return to you weeping,
    mending our ways, seeking your advice to change our habits,
    you hear us coming from afar. Even before our words are
    audible you rush to our comfort,
        scooping us up eagerly like lost children, found.
        You carry us home. Nursing, you nourish us,
            filling us full until we become like a child,
            weaned and content, resting on its mother's lap.
For all your universal wonders, we praise you.
For all your showering benefits, we thank you.
For all your daily miracles, we murmur gratitude.
Generation after generation you continue blessing.
You are the rock we grasp and hold.

You are the shield we lift for protection.
Age upon age you remain steadfast.

At all times and seasons,
in all places and persons,
we see and hear and feel
the goodness of your presence.

"Blessed are you, Giving God,
Benefactor of Heaven and Earth in every age.
Your name is Generosity.
You convey wonder and miracle day after day
to the earth and its people.
To you we lift our hearts and voices
in this prayer of gratitude."

Magnificat of Peace

Gratitude is the fruit of my soul.
    Praise my sustenance.
Thankfulness is the song of my spirit.
    Fidelity my nourishment.
O Holy One of Many Blessings, we ask one blessing more.
    Grant us peace.
    Grant us a goodly peace,
        kind and compassionate.
    Grant a just peace to us, to all Israel, your people,
        and to all the righteous of your world.
    Bless us our Father, all of us gathered here together
        like a family clustered around its mother's table.
    We stand quiet in your holiness.

In ancient times you empowered your faithful to extend their hands
over one another in the wilderness, giving voice to your promise of
blessed assurance, saying,
    "The Living God blesses you and keeps you tenderly.
    The Living God casts forth light upon you,
        granting you graciousness.
    The Living God lifts up to you a sacred presence
        and places before you, peace."

"Blessed are you, our Truth and our Promise,
    We who bear your name receive your blessing.
    We who are blessed by you carry forth your peace."

PART THREE: DAILY LIVING

"The attraction of people is their kindness.

The listening heart and the watchful spirit,

the Living God has made them both."

TEACHINGS FOR MY CHILDREN

Miryam speaks:
What is a sage?
>A sage is one who does the will of God because of love.

Who is a son of God? Who is God's daughter?
>The heirs of God are those who serve God.

>The offspring of God are those who love mightily and live kindly lives. God's children turn toward goodness, searching, like babes at the breast nourished, weaned on the love of God.

>The generations of God are the ones who return.

Who are the tainted ones?
>The tainted ones are those who preach beautifully
>>but do not act beautifully.

>They are seekers after smooth things.

Why do our people tell stories?
>We tell stories because the Torah tells us that the
>teachings of God will flow forth on a flood of talk,
>carried along in a rush of delight.

In the days when we first began telling our stories, people
>gathered round fires, clustered in caves and in tents.

In those days we began speaking of Wisdom, who God created even
>before the separation of the waters. Her teachings were
>called by the name Justice.

>>Then the earth cried out, "Do not leave us in the rule of
>>justice alone, for you have created your people for

choosing. Your people will sometimes choose to drink the
waters of turning away. Do not leave us in the rule of
justice alone, let mercy be ours also."
God said, "Amen. So shall it be in my reign forever. Justice
and mercy shall be companions. And the name of my reign
shall be called Righteousness."
In this way repentance and restoration were created in the moment
the world began. The first call of God was "Return."

Now we tell stories of return
        catching a glimpse of the world to come
        when all peoples shall be returned,
        justice and mercy ruling together
                in a reign called Righteousness.
Then people will sing praises all through the day
        and lay down at night in peace
                to receive the messengers of God.
The stories of sages will be told everywhere,
        uniting heaven and earth in joy.
        No one on all God's Holy Mountain will know fear
        because we will not harm one another.
We tell stories now so that all may return
        and hasten the day of the world to come.

THESE ARE THE THINGS WE DID

Miryam speaks:

For forty days, Jesus, whom God had revived from death, taught the Eleven. We waited in Jerusalem for the promise Jesus often taught about, the promise of an encounter with the Holy Spirit.

When we were together, some had asked him, "Is it time now?"

Jesus responded, "It is not for you to know the exact date and time. These are God's alone. It is for you to be receptive to the power of the Spirit of God when it comes upon you, and then to go out and bear witness with your lives according to what I have taught you. Begin here in Jerusalem, and then throughout Judea and Samaria, and even away to the end of the earth."

There on the Mount of Olives, facing the Temple, God lifted him up. The cloud of God covered him. We returned within Jerusalem's walls directly to the upper rooms where we had been staying. The followers organized the band according to the way of the twelve tribes. There were the eleven plus another whom Jesus had taught, called apostles, as well as many devout men and women, nearly one hundred and twenty Jews and their families, known as disciples. Jacob the kinsman — in Greek, James — led us all.

We continued watching in prayer. These days after Passover are the days of counting. It is written in the Torah, "And you shall count for yourselves from the morrow after the Sabbath that you brought the omer-barley from the sheaves of the wave-offering."

Day by day we counted from the feast of remembering God bringing us forth from Egypt, seven weeks of counting days. We waited as

Jerusalem filled up with pilgrims for the Feast of Weeks. On the fiftieth day, the day the Greeks call Pentecost, we celebrate the giving of the Torah at Mount Sinai. In each home and synagogue and from the Temple steps we accept again God's teachings, our ancient covenant.

On the fiftieth day, we began with evening prayer and in the city all through the night we Jews studied Torah. We were gathered for morning prayer and the day was running its course. The texts we read from the scrolls recalled the lightning over Sinai on this great day and then the prophet Ezekiel's fiery vision of God's throne. And in the midst of it all, God's fiery Spirit came also to us, and we were enspirited as in days of old. We went out into the streets. Because of the Pentecost celebration there were people from every land milling around in Jerusalem, devout Jews, non-observant Jews, proselytes, God-fearers, visitors, soldiers, traders and merchants from Mesopotamia and Rome, Libya, and Egypt up to Syria and Macedonia.

We were filled with the Holy Spirit and our words poured forth like a flood. All who heard us understood what we said, even those from diverse places. Like Hannah, we appeared drunken. People were amazed.

We were set alight according to the prophecy of Joel, "sons and daughters prophesying, old and young dreaming visions." God's Spirit poured out upon us. We told of the wonders of God in our lives and we spoke of the teacher we follow — Jesus, the man from Nazareth. From that day on we were called Nazarenes.

Cephas, the one the Greeks call Peter, issued forth the call, following in Jesus' footsteps. "Repent, repent, enter the cleansing waters and accept God's forgiveness. Receive God's fiery Spirit."

Those who were sinners among them, many from corrupt and rebellious places, heard him and wept, repenting of their ways. We went to the waters with them and they entered and accepted cleansing. They turned toward God. Many came, many beyond counting, all wanting leadership from us, wanting to follow the teacher from Nazareth. So we organized a common life.

They came every day to hear the witnesses teach. Our houses of gathering were filled. People gave alms, some tithing, some giving all, and we prayed and shared table fellowship together, blessing God for everything.

A sense of awe was among us. Our spirits were lifted up by all that happened, flying like eagles on the wing.

All those who had made a commitment to follow the teachings of the Nazarene held their lives in common, distributing to one another according to their need. With one heart we kept daily attendance at the Temple, lived in joy and simplicity, and were well liked by the people of Jerusalem, both Jews and pagans.

Those whom Jesus had taught, taught others. On the edge of Temple Mount, in the walkway called Solomon's Porch, they shared what they had learned. Men and women, Gentile and Jew, could listen to their story. When healing was asked for, it was given. The followers preached truthfully:

"We have no power, no holiness ourselves. The God of Abraham, the God of Isaac, the God of Jacob heals you. This God of our ancestors restored Jesus, servant of God. Some of your Sadducean officials made a mock trial under the cover of night, cooperating in the Roman Game of Kings, saying, 'It is expedient that one man should die for the people than that the whole nation should perish.' They took him from Caiaphas to Herod to Pilate, who washed his hands of blood guilt and gave him over to the legionnaires to play with. Corrupting a choice into no choice at all, the Sadducees conspired for the people's own vote to betray him. Even before this, we, his own followers, had fled in fear. We betrayed Jesus and we were not present in the voting crowd to support him.

"The Roman legionnaires dressed him up like a king, put him on a throne, wrapped him in a purple gown, set a crown upon him.

Jeering and mocking, smearing him with spit and filth, they paraded him through the streets up the hill and crucified him. They nailed the name of their game at the head of his cross, 'King, King of the Jews,' and they gambled away his garments.

"But from the violence of dark conspiracies and disciples' betrayal, God redeemed him. The Living God brings forth life from death. What began in humiliation has ended in glory.

"Those of us who are wicked can know forgiveness and become heirs to the prophets."

Some Sadducees, Herod's High Priest, and a Temple commander of the guard overheard them in Solomon's Portico. They came and arrested them. The next day these, and a collection of the Friends of the King who had handed over Jesus, examined them. They were exasperated that untrained laymen were expounding in the Temple. Then they recognized them as followers of Jesus the Nazarene. But this time the followers were unafraid of priestly power. They stood boldly teaching sound Torah values, and the tribunal had no choice but to discharge them.

They returned to us, told us their story, and we gave thanks for what had happened. As we ended our prayer, the house trembled. We were filled with God's presence. Teaching continually, boldly urged by God's Spirit, we ran and did not grow weary.

We who followed Jesus were united, one in heart and one in soul. None of us, not one, claimed ownership of anything. The community held everything and no one among us was ever in need. Thereby we gained the respect of both residents and visitors in Jerusalem.

We continued to meet near Solomon's Porch. Because of those who were eyes and ears for Caiaphas, it was dangerous, and others did not join us there. But outside, on the streets of Jerusalem, many sinners came, men and women. They brought people for healing. They repented, returning to God and setting out on a life of kindness.

Again some among us were arrested. Herod's High Priest and his henchmen and some Sadducees took them in custody. One of God's angels caused their release in the night. The next day our people came to the Temple at daybreak when prayers began. They prayed and taught as usual in the same spot. The High Priest and his cadre convened the entire Sanhedrin. This was the full court of Israel. Though Herod had put to death forty-five Pharisees, some men of integrity still served among them. Those of us found teaching were arrested and brought before the Council.

Herod's High Priest confronted them, "We ordered you to stop teaching in that name. Why didn't you stop? You fill Jerusalem with your teaching and accuse us of responsibility for that man's death."

Peter spoke for everyone, "We must obey God rather than human beings. The God of our ancestors redeemed Jesus. You and your henchmen cooperated in allowing the Roman soldiers to humiliate and crucify him. God, who restored him as a right-hand servant, leads us and saves us. God grants us repentance and forgiveness in Israel. We are witnesses to this and to the Holy Spirit given by God."

This enraged their accusers, who wished them dead.

Then there rose up in the Sanhedrin a Pharisee called Gamaliel, God Redeems Me. A teacher of Torah, he was held in great respect by all the people. Gamaliel moved that our people be sent outside for a time and he addressed the Sanhedrin.

"Court of Israel, be careful in what you decide to do regarding these people." He gave examples of other leaders who had risen and fallen. Then he advised them, "Stay away from these people. I say to you, leave them alone! If this teaching of theirs is of human origin, it will die its own death. However, if it is of God, it will live. You cannot defeat it. And you risk being remembered as men who opposed the will of God."

The Sanhedrin respected Gamaliel's words. But the henchmen flogged our people, which only increased our zeal.

Every day, day after day, we went steadily on with the teaching. We learned and prayed together and lived according to Torah as taught by Moses, our sages, and our beloved Jesus. All the while we heard rumors of the brilliant Saul of Tarsus who had come to Jerusalem seeking knowledge of Jewish teaching. How much time he spent attending the classes of Gamaliel's school, we did not know, but he had left there and was now persecuting us for Caiaphas. We then heard that he had extended his operations all the way up to Damascus. Passports there could only be secured through Herod's henchmen.

On the way to Damascus one day, he had an experience of light, and turned toward our teachings. Saul took on the name of Paul and spent several years learning, repenting, making amends, and accepting forgiveness before returning to teach in the gentile world.

The congregations in Jerusalem, throughout Judea, Samaria, and Galilee were left in peace to grow strong. We worship together with devout Jews who live Torah as taught by other teachers. In some places we have our own houses. We stand like Adam and Eve, like the matriarchs and patriarchs, like the people's priest in the Holy of Holies, always in awe of God. Sustained by the Spirit, we become strong.

There are problems and pains, arguments and differences. We continue our acts of feeding the poor and seeing to the needs of our own. Herod has not ceased his violent persecutions. Murder and arrest are ever present, with all Jews living under the threats day and night. But the work to which we are called continues.

The Jerusalem congregation led by James, our kinsman, guides the growing movement according to the teachings of Moses. Paul contends with us sorely from his outposts in the gentile world. He wants changes in the way of life to accommodate the pagan followers. It is an agonizing issue. We want to live as we lived with Jesus while he was among us. But Paul has so many who want to congregate according to his own teachings. He urges us with cogent arguments that changes will hasten the day of the world to come.

We compromise, but James makes clear that these converted pagans must at least live righteous lives. As in the Torah, Jews are to remain Jews and gentiles are to follow the mandates given to Noah after the flood. These commands Moses our teacher passed on to us. Those who are not circumcised, who do not bear the sacred seal of covenant in their flesh, must live lives of righteousness. They are to refrain from the idolatry and promiscuity so rampant in their world. They must eat only meat that has been mercifully slaughtered and prepared according to the laws of purity, prepared with gratitude to the one Living God. A portion of everything must be given to the poor. They must not shed blood.

Because of all these issues we are called in Rome, "the Church of the Circumcised and the Church of the Gentiles," but pagan Romans simply know us as devout Jews. Our care for the community is respected and our joy attracts many in Rome. However, Roman legionnaires who knew us from their service in Israel continue their cruelty, spreading mischief and lies.

The community here in Jerusalem remains strong, even though beset by testing and tragedy. The evil Herod killed our beloved leader, James, but we have his witness in writing and share it everywhere. Cephas joined Saul in Rome, where they labor to establish the teachings of Jesus in the gentile world. I spent much time teaching them here in Jerusalem before they left, and they use this fact as a source of authority to the Romans. Peter must overcome the stain of his public betrayal. Paul, of course, never knew Jesus at all.

My work continues. Like my kinswomen, I am strong and vital in old age. We are writing things down, of course, especially collections of teachings and stories of remembrances. They seem to go out as quickly as our scribes record them, some carried east and some carried west.

The Roman Legions are a menace, and day by day we grow more apprehensive here in our holy city. We have already sent some with records into the hills for safety. I hope they survive so that our true story will be told.

I fear for Jerusalem. Like my son, I love her dearly. She is the heart of Israel. I long to protect her, to hold her to my breast and shield her as a mother shields an infant. Thoughts that Rome will harm her ancient beauty, her devout population, and our Temple fill me with sorrow. O Jerusalem, where so many gifts of the Living God have settled upon us, I see lecherous armies gathered around you. I see your fragility and I weep.

(retold in the Acts of the Apostles)

REPENT AND BELIEVE

Miryam speaks:
"Prepare a way in the wilderness,
      clear before God a straight path."
      Isaiah calls.
      The devout of Israel come.
"Repent. Confess your sins, for the time is soon."
      John, who baptizes, echoes Isaiah.
      Many Jews who have fallen away return.
"The time is now, the reign of God very near at hand.
      Repent and believe the good news."
      Jesus of Nazareth summons,
      and some come who have never come before.

Jesus taught, saying, "I come not for the righteous, but for the wicked,
not for the healthy, but for the sick. I come not for the flock of Israel,
but for the lost sheep."

What does it mean . . . repent, believe, return, and live?
      Israel's way of repentance is this:
      Every day in prayer and deed, we return.
      Every month at the Feast of New Moon, we return.
      Every year at the Day of Atonement, we return.
      Every year after seven times seven years, in the 50th year,
            we declare a Year of Jubilee and we return.
And every seventh day, from evening until evening, we confirm our belief that the reign of God is among us. Resting, we celebrate a day when
heaven and earth are at one. We anticipate the Great Day of Sabbath.
      Israel's way to repent and believe is to awaken continual con-
sciousness. Come, let me teach you our way of devotion.

First, cease the busyness. Be still. Look at life.
    Awake and arouse.
    You who have fallen asleep in life, get up!
    Flee from forgetting. Refuse to be numb.
We ask ourselves the questions that God asked Hagar.
    "Where have you been?
    Where are you going?"
We look at the route we have traveled. Are we running away?
    Have we missed the mark?
    Have we knowingly continued on the wrong road?
    Have we planned and pursued a crooked path?

I am a person, created free by God's design.
By my own will, I lean toward God or not.
No force yokes me to the careless and deceitful.
I am not by nature evil-bent.

Where I have missed the mark,
I now look clearly at the target,
    sizing my error, admitting my mistakes, voicing remorse,
    making amends.
I mark the course true again.

When I have knowingly continued on the wrong road,
I honestly survey God's map,
    assessing, revealing, grieving, repairing, resolving, redirecting.
I seek my way again.

However I have planned and pursued a crooked path,
I humbly seek a true one.
    Recalling each betrayal, exposing hardened habits, bit by
    bit I set about the lengthy task of change, mending stitch

by stitch, resetting stone by stone, lamenting, re-forming,
    redesigning the fabric of my life.
I clear before God a straight path.

God holds the course when we return to the teachings;
    the world can be healed in our hands.
God welcomes stable minds and acts of amending.
God rejoices, delights in our steps of return.
The gate is always open, the cup always full.
        Pardon is our drink. Salvation is our bread,
            and our bread is named Freedom,
                the freedom to choose freedom again and again.
No matter how bitter the taste of failure,
    there's a cloying sweetness to sin.
There is an allure to never being responsible,
    to blaming another for all that occurs,
    to working on someone else's time.

O God, our God, we come to you.
    We come singing words of our desert wedding . . .
    "I am my beloved's and my beloved is mine."
Holy One, we are truly sorry,
    we have made amends and planned our new direction.
    Accept us. Return us and we shall be returned again.
    From hardness of heart and arrogance, we return.
    From hopelessness, cynicism and violence, we return.
    From gossip, gloating, and tale bearing, we return.
    From failed promises and taking more than our share, we return.
    From holding back loving kindness,
        from laxness in learning your teaching,
        from enticing others to waste or reject,
        from discouraging words, we return.

From confessing our sins with our mouths alone,
    refusing to change or repay,
    from all these and more, we return.
Before you we lift our eyes in naked admission,
    raise our empty hands in poverty of gift.
        Tears are our lot. Weeping our substance.
You, creator of the universe, are the Living God.
    You are the One who inhabits our heart.
    You suffer when we ignore you.
    You cry out in pain when our tongue afflicts a loved one.
You hunger when we fail to search day and night to feed the
    hungry. You groan when we forget your teachings, weep when
    we break promises.
Ashamed, filled with remorse, we stand before you.
You are not without pity,
    neither can you be tricked or purchased.
Ritual without heart, without mind, without strength
    is contemptible to you.
We come to the lively waters of rebirth, returning.
    "Blessed are you, creator and source of all things,
    who teaches us to immerse ourselves in cleansing waters."

Your right hand of justice sets our feet firmly on the straight way. Your
left hand of mercy lifts up our heads and wipes away our guilt. In a
clean vessel in God's house, we too shall live.

(retold in the gospel of Mark)

My Son Is the Gate

Miryam speaks:
There is a Garden and God rests within it.
The soil is fertile. The weeds are few.
The vines growing there bear fruit.
The Garden is tended by long-time laborers.
Workers taught a particular way.
They graft and prune, sow and harvest, water and drain,
day and night according to teachings offered them by God
once long ago in the wilderness.

These teachings they accept, bind to themselves, treasure, and
pass on from generation to generation. They live by and die because
of these teachings — writ on a sacred scroll by their own hand in their
own language. These bonded-workers, faithful through time, are dear to
the heart of God, and God is dear to the hearts of these laborers.

Through the years together, they've built a fence, encompassing
them and their teachings, a kindly fence and strong, to hold them secure and keep the wondering from wandering, a firm fence that defines
their grove and separates them from others and others from them.

The world looking on from outside is wary.
Do you wish to work in the Garden of God?
The workers will willingly teach you their way,
    provided you show you are earnest.
    Turning toward God, you may enter through fresh running
    rivers. They will lead you.

Perhaps their way is not your way . . . what then?
 Are you forever shut out of the Garden?
The ancient workers say that there are other ways to enter.
 The harvest is plentiful. Workers are wanted.

My Son is a Gate, through him you may enter.
My Son is a Way, follow him.
 He will lead you to an orchard and help you to harvest.
 He will give you an acre and teach you to plant.
It is well to remember,
 In God's Garden there are many groves,
 each one tended in the way God intends,
 and the name of God's Garden is Peace.

There is a Pasture where God roams.
 In these valleys and hills an ancient flock flourishes,
 a flock with ways of its own.
 You may join that flock through the meadow stream,
 and learning its age-old customs,
 graze and frolic among them.
 Perhaps you don't know their meadow,
 you find the crags unfamiliar and steep.
My Son will shepherd you. Come, follow him.
My Son will guard you, holding you like a lamb in his arms.
 In God's Pasture there are many meadows,
 each one tended in the way God intends,
 and the name of God's Pasture is Peace.

There is a Household where God dwells
 attended by friends old and new.

In this House there are guests, whomever God chooses.

God sends out word. By invitation God gathers in. Each moment from dawning to dawning, faithful retainers serve the repast, they dance and sing to their ancient tunes.

You too may learn to serve with them.

Perhaps your way of service is different.

My Son is a Word inviting you in.

He is Light lighting your way.

My Son is Bread at the Banquet.

In God's Household there are many dwelling rooms.

Each tended as God intends,

and the name of God's Household is Peace.

There is a Heaven where God resides,

many among us come and go.

Once on a Galilean hill a young Jew named Jacob laid himself down to rest. Using a stone for a pillow, he fell asleep. Dreaming a dream, he saw a ladder, set up on the earth. It reached into the heavens. Angels of God were ascending and descending upon it and God stood above it at the very opening to heaven. God spoke words of promise and blessing to Jacob.

According to the promise, God accompanies the family of Jacob forever, always observing the way of the world, seeing, sustaining, judging, regarding how others regard this holy beloved people.

You too may become a source of promise and blessing.

You too may be kept by God.

My Son is a Witness. He sees into your heart even as you stand beneath
a fig tree in the distance. He knows your worth.

My Son is a Ladder, set upon the earth reaching into the heavens.

All those God sends to my Son shall come and he will not cast them aside.

But none can come to him unless God chooses to draw them there. You too will become a holy and beloved people whom God accompanies observing the way of the world, seeing, sustaining, judging, regarding how others regard you.

Into the Heaven where God resides there are many ladders
each tended as God intends,
and the name of God's Heaven is Peace.

My Son is God's gift. What is it you long for?
    He is the Gate for those without a gate,
        the Way for those who do not know the way,
        a shepherd and guard for all of his sheep.
    My Son is the Word of invitation to the Banquet,
        Light and Bread for all his friends.
    My Son is the Ladder, all those who come to the Father
        through him, come this way.

(retold in the gospel of John)

One Hundred Blessings a Day

Miryam speaks:
O Holy One of Blessing,
    I will lift up my thoughts to you.
        I will cherish you in my heart and recognize your wonders.
          Only then will the words of blessing cross my lips.
          No blessing can dwell where love is absent.

Daily we gather for meals.
    It is written: "They gazed on God, they ate and they drank."
    "Blessed are you, Loving God, Maker who sustains the world,
        who creates the fruit of the vine."
    "Blessed are you, Teaching God, Master of the Universe,
        who teaches us to wash our hands."
    "Blessed are you, Living God, Creator of all things,
        who brings forth bread from the Land."

Regard yourself as though the entire earth depended upon you.
    To save one life is to preserve a generation.
    One caring action lifts up the whole world.
    With one blessing, much is blessed.
    With one word of thanks, there is increasing gratitude.

No blessing can dwell where love is absent.
What we live defines what we believe.
"Blessed are you Eternal, source of all wisdom in the world,
    who creates fragrant trees, seeds, grasses, flowers,

who creates fragrant herbs, edible fruits and nuts,
who places enticing aroma into blossoms
and makes them all delightful to the eye."

Do not make of your prayers a fixed thing.
Let new meaning rise up from the love of your heart,
from the work of your hands,
and from the thoughts of your mind.

"Blessed are you, Beloved Mystery,
you are the one who spoke
and all things began to happen."
You teach us that you are hidden.
You teach us that you are revealed.

The person who receives from God without uttering a blessing,
that person is a thief.
The one who tastes, who sees, who hears and touches,
who inhales a fragrance without pouring out the water of
their soul upon it,
that one steals from God.

The person who delights in the pulse of the body,
who construes an inventive thought,
who laughs with a kindred spirit,
and infuses it not with the breath of blessing,
that person lessens the Reign of God.

No blessing can dwell where love is absent.
What we live defines what we believe.
We come together at times and seasons.
"Blessed are you, who has kept us alive to this season."

"Blessed are you who heals what is past."
At the first of each month, we attend like a family at a
birthing as the slim thread of light crescents the moon.
We envision new opportunities for justice,
    for thoughtfulness,
    for faithfulness and gratitude.

As an infant pure and full of promise signs new beginnings,
    so does the new moon, so also each blossom, each kiss.
    Cradle them all, lift them up in the way of righteousness,
      and their name shall be called "Hope."
"Blessed are you, Creator of the Signs and Wonders
    throughout heaven and earth."

You strengthen us, filling the world with your power. Gratitude and
amazement fire our faith. Let us infuse creation with God's mercy, im-
press creation with God's might.
    Bless, I say, and bless again.
    One hundred times each day ignite the world with gratitude.

(retold in the gospel of Luke)

WE REMEMBER THE NIGHT AND THE MORNING

Miryam speaks:
Knowledge, faith, and freedom to choose God.
Without these three, we are little more than beasts of the field.
With these three, we are but little less than angels.

In each time people must struggle.
     Knowledge, faith, and freedom are in each season verified.
     Each person, each people, make choices in a lifetime.
In every age there are betrayers.
     Men trade honor for ease.
     Women surrender wisdom for comfort.
     Teachers press students for payment.
     Priests sell services to the poor.
     Scholars exchange integrity for titles.
     Youth are contaminated by gaudiness.
And yet in the midst of it all many are righteous.
Even in seasons of terror, times of sequestered scrolls and whispered blessings, kindly deeds in silence done, even then, the love of God burns on.

"God of Hosts, Holy Warrior,
     may we become zealots for you in our time."

In a world where there is fateful confusion,
     where purveyors of violence plan and stalk,
     may we know the difference between
          the stranger and the enemy.
May the light of your teachings reveal your true meaning.
     As we stand at the banquet of choices, God,
          let it be with a listening heart.
     Teach us to be as you recommend.
God, let us be wise as serpents, gentle as doves.

Help us to face your terrible knowledge,
     "There may be people with whom you cannot stand.
     Even though you come with willing spirit,
          my covenant clutched to your breast,
          you must recognize the law which binds the other."
Help us to listen well to the other . . .
     near and far, past and now.
     It may be there is no hope for solidarity.
     It may be our covenants conflict.
     Only where there is commitment to life can people stand together.
The prophets have warned us. Dare we not listen?
     "There are those who corrupt covenants, flattered by titles and
fame. But you, my people, you are to act with wisdom, causing many
to understand. Even so, prepare yourselves for struggle, to suffer the
stone and the flame, to endure threat and captivity. People in tempo-
ral power honor gods of fortresses and money and use unbelievers to
defend them. They confer honors and authority and divide the land for
a price. Yet those who are corrupt, whose judgments are crooked and
whose mercies are traps, these shall come to an end. There will be no
one to help them. Then they that are wise shall illumine the firmament,
and they that turn the many to justice and mercy shall shine as the stars
forever."

Knowledge, faith, and freedom to choose God.
Without these three, we are little more than beasts of the field.
With these three, we are little less than angels.

(letters from Jerusalem to the Gentiles)

The Day of the World to Come

Miryam speaks:
God created us for life.
    Woman and man, dynamic Likeness of the Living One,
    standing now in Jerusalem,
    called with Abraham and Sarah,
    redeemed with Moses, Aaron, and Miryam,
    restored with Ezra, prophets and teachers,
    disciples of Jesus, the Nazarene,
        God's servant whom we follow,
    this is our hope for the world to come.
Everywhere on earth strangers will settle side by side,
    one shall not oppress the other,
    both shall be as native born,
    loving one another as they love themselves,
        because we have all been strangers.
No one will be reduced to poverty.
    Each and all will work, earnestly,
        increasing trust and bread,
    little by little drawing the world toward goodness,
    repairing the aching, bleeding, beloved earth.
Women and men alone with children will declare their real needs,
    and be recognized,
    the sick we will heal, the grieving comfort,
    the old we will make young at heart.

Nations will change themselves, turning to God.
    Each people will be holy
        according to God's teachings to them,
           and we will respect one another.
Everyone will choose to lean toward justice,
    to embrace compassion as a way of life.
Deeds of loving kindness will become the norm.

    Abundant herbs and grain, fruit, and produce will be cultivated.
Each tiller will take what is required, distributing to the helpless, leaving a generous portion in the field for the poor and the stranger to gather, and there will be plenty to store up for winter.
God will be praised at every table,
    liturgy and prayer enriching our homes.
They will be places
    of laughter, merriment and hospitality,
    places congenial to work and friendship.
Our homes will be houses of study,
    where God's teachings are sought and discerned.
Kindled lights will grace our window. Then we will celebrate and
    each soul will have cause for celebration,
    each soul, the wherewithal to feast.
Then earth will be a sanctuary,
    where everything is holy, all are safe,
    the wicked not destroyed, but turned from their ways alive.
Then we who have all labored together shall rest.

This time will be called the Great Sabbath,
    the Age of the Messiah,
    the Day of the World to Come.
"O Living, Loving God,
    lifted up and hallowed be your name,

may your will be done.
May your reign be revealed.
May it happen soon.
    Quickly.
    Now in our time.
        Amen."

(ancient teachings recorded as revelation)

EPILOGUE

Together we have told the stories, prayed the prayers, and considered the teachings of the Jerusalem community. What are the church's teachings today and how does Mary teach us now?

The church's directives are clear. The Vatican II document *Nostra Aetate* (1965) directs us to cease the teachings of contempt regarding the Jewish people, which include specifically the charge of deicide. Further documents such as *Guidelines for Implementation of Nostra Aetate* (1975), *Notes on the Presentation of Jews and Judaism in Preaching and Catechesis* (1985), and the *U.S. Catholic Bishops' Guidelines* (current) detail specific criteria.

Bishops and theologians continue to interpret and direct these developments. The work of Dr. Eugene Fisher, of the Secretariat for Catholic-Jewish Relations of the National Conference of Catholic Bishops; Dr. John Pawlikowski, OSM, Professor at the Catholic Theological Union, Chicago; Dr. Martin Hengle, Professor of New Testament and Early Judaism in the University of Tubingen; and Bishop Kirster Stendahl of Harvard and Stockholm, Sweden, is long standing.

John Pawlikowski transmits the directives issued by the 1985 *Notes* as follows: to build a positive theology of Judaism from a typological base, to moderate, albeit implicitly, any absolutist claims about the Christian faith and to become a faithful witness to the *"Notes'* startling assertion that Jews and Christians are indispensable partners in human redemption."

In the United States, the Catholic bishops have implemented the directives in their pastoral letter on the American economy and in directives to priests and catechists on the Lenten readings. The directives from the dioceses of Los Angeles, Newark, and Louisville are particularly helpful. I have used this body of material in writing the entire text, and it is especially evident in the final section, *Daily Living*.

Mary's directives are equally clear. The church has maintained a tradition over the centuries of Mary's continual teaching presence. Believing witnesses treasure and record her words to her vision-struck children and celebrate their vitality. From Fatima and Lourdes, from Guadalupe and Medjugorje, Mary stands teaching those who have ears to hear her. She teaches Christians to fast and pray, repent, convert their hearts and lives, return to the traditions taught by her Son, renew faithfulness in the church, and pursue peace and justice at home and in their own Christian environment. She has never stopped teaching. Her lessons seem concerned with our validity as living witnesses to a gospel of love and with the church's integrity as the vessel of her Son's ministry. Jesus taught, "Remove the log in your own eye before noticing the small splinter in the eye of another."

I experience a remarkable convergence in the teachings of Mary and in the church directives. I have reached for this renewing church tradition in the creation of this text. This original imperative to pursue peace first in our Mother's household has been my inspiration.

The church and its Mother are teaching us again. The church was born to bring forth bread and life from its own resources to offer as balm for an aching world. It is not for us to demean the neighbor we are commanded to love, even for a heartfelt reason. Hating is not healthy and we were created for wholeness and joy.

On April 13, 1986, Pope John Paul II stood on the steps of the Main Synagogue together with Chief Rabbi of Rome Elio Toaff. He called to mind the vital Jewish community that had lived in Rome since one hundred years before the birth of Jesus. He voiced this intention for the Roman Catholic church: "To overcome old prejudices and secure ever wider and fuller recognition of that 'bond' and that 'common spiritual patrimony' that exists between Jews and Christians."

He reminded us of the extent of the work accomplished by his predecessors and asked that all present and all people of the church "underline" these points:

The first is that the Church of Christ discovers her bond with Judaism by "searching into her own mystery." The Jewish religion is not "extrinsic" to our own religion. You (the Jews he is addressing) are our dearly beloved brothers and, in a certain way, it could be said that you are our elder brothers.

The second point noted by the Council is that no ancestral or collective blame can be imputed to the Jews as a people for "what happened in Christ's passion." Not indiscriminately to the Jews of that time, nor to those who came afterwards, nor to those of today. So any alleged theological justification for discriminatory measures or, worse still, for acts of persecution is unfounded. The Lord will judge each one "according to his own works," Jews and Christians alike.

The third point that I would like to emphasize in the Council's Declaration is a consequence of the second. Notwithstanding the Church's awareness of her own identity, it is not lawful to say that the Jews are "repudiated or cursed," as if this were taught or could be deduced from the Sacred Scriptures of the Old or the New Testament.

Referring to the text of *Nostra Aetate* and also the Dogmatic Constitution *Lumen Gentium,* the pope said, "the Jews are beloved of God, who has called them with an irrevocable calling" (Letter to the Romans).

He noted that the "path undertaken is still at the beginning" and would take "time and great effort to remove all forms of prejudice, even subtle ones, to readjust every manner of self-expression and therefore to present always and everywhere to ourselves and to others, the true face of the Jews and Judaism as likewise Christians and of Christianity, and this at every level of outlook, teaching and communication."

He reminded "all my brothers and sisters of the Catholic Church of the guidelines for implementing the Vatican Council in this precise field as already available in documents of 1974 and 1985 by the Holy See's Commission for Religious Relations with Judaism." He instructs us, "It is only a question of studying them carefully, of immersing oneself in their teachings and of putting them into practice."

The pope ended his remarks with a psalm "in its original language which is also your [the Jews'] inheritance." He then prayed the psalm in Hebrew.

This book is a contribution to that directive of the church. I hope the work of storytellers and poets can add a bit to the work of theologians and translators, that together we can recover and extend to the world community the great message of peace and justice that has been entrusted to Christians by Jesus.